IT'S ALL ABOUT MILLIMETERS

HOW SMALL CHANGES CAN MAKE A BIG IMPACT IN YOUR BUSINESS AND YOUR LIFE

DR. DONNA GALANTE

Copyright © 2013 by Dr. Donna Galante. All rights reserved. No part of this book may be reproduced or transmitted in any form or by any means, electronic or mechanical, including photocopying, recording or by any information storage and retrieval system, without the written permission of the publisher except in the case of brief quotations or except where permitted by law.

The information contained in this book is intended to be educational and not for diagnosis, prescription or treatment of any health disorder whatsoever. This book is sold with the understanding that neither the author nor publisher is engaged in rendering any legal, psychological or accounting advice. The publisher and author disclaim personal liability, directly or indirectly, for advice of information presented within. Although the author and publisher have prepared this manuscript with utmost care and diligence and have made every effort to ensure the accuracy and completeness of the information contained within, we assume no responsibility for errors, inaccuracies, omissions or inconsistencies.

Library of Congress Control Number: 2013939321
ISBN-13: 9780989136013
It's All About Millimeters Softcover Edition 2013
Printed in the United States of America

For more information about special discounts for bulk purchases, please contact 3L Publishing at 916.300.8012 or log onto our website at www.3LPublishing.com.

Book design by Erin Pace-Molina
Cover image from Shutterstock.com
Author image photograph by Gail Shoop-Lamy

To Paul, Carina and Nate

CONTENTS

1   INTRODUCTION

PART 1: IT'S ALL ABOUT MILLIMETERS AND YOUR BUSINESS

7   Chapter 1: What is the Millimeter Approach to Business and Life?

15   Chapter 2: Why Millimeters Matter So Much in Your Business

27   Chapter 3: Using Millimeters in Your Hiring Process

35   Chapter 4: Millimeter Businesses Focus on the "Three Ts"

45   Chapter 5: A Millimeter Approach to Your Systems and Procedures

53   Chapter 6: Marketing with Millimeter Precision

65   Chapter 7: Make Your Patients, Clients and Customers Members of AA

77   Chapter 8: Educating Potential Customers, Clients and Patients is a Top Priority of a Millimeter Business

87   Chapter 9: Millimeter Businesses Focus on Exceptional Experiences

PART 2: IT'S ALL ABOUT MILLIMETERS AND LIFE

99   Chapter 10: A Millimeter Approach to Leadership

109   Chapter 11: Millimeters and Time Management Equals Powerful Personal Productivity

121   Chapter 12: A Millimeter Approach to Relationships

135   Chapter 13: A Millimeter Approach to Health and Wellness

147   Chapter 14: Changing Your Mindset with a Millimeter Approach

155   **CONCLUSION**

159   **ACKNOWLEDGMENTS**

163   **ABOUT THE AUTHOR**

INTRODUCTION

*"All of our dreams can come true —
if we have the courage to pursue them."*
— Walt Disney

I have a confession to make to you. I am an orthodontist, not an MBA, not an attorney, and not an accountant. I do not hold undergraduate degrees in business. Why I wanted to confess this right upfront is because you will be reading a book about goals achieved in millimeters. As an orthodontist or anyone in the dental profession will tell you, we measure our success by millimeters, which is how I've come to look at things not only in business but also in life.

I might be exaggerating a bit about size, but millimeters while small are mighty powerful in our professional results. For example, in orthodontics, a millimeter discrepancy in the final position of a tooth could mean a less-than-perfect bite, less-than-perfect alignment, and less-than-perfect smile. Dental professionals are detail-oriented — and a millimeter is a big deal. If a single tooth still needs a millimeter of forward movement, it can look like a foot or yard out of place. A millimeter opening in a filling will allow bacteria to enter the tooth and can cause further damage. Too many millimeters of "pocket" depth around a tooth could compromise it long term. So in my profession, millimeters are very important in terms of our professional results.

I use the metaphor of millimeters to share with you, the reader, how small steps, changes and actions can make a BIG difference in the results you try to achieve. Too many people take the all-or-nothing approach (aka "cold turkey") to achieve a goal or promise that they have made. My premise is to take a different approach — the millimeter method to use to make a change, take action and get results. Instead of waking up tomorrow and saying, "I am going to lose 10 pounds this week," why not try the millimeter approach? For example, I say, "I am going to lose one pound a week for 10 weeks using this diet plan versus 50 pounds in a year."

In my coaching business, I often coach my dentist clients that instead of building out the Taj Mahal of dental offices and going into stressful debt burdens, why not start off with a very nice, clean, modern office? Why buy new when you can invest in perfectly acceptable used equipment and furniture? I advise them to limit their debt to the most minimal amount possible, which is how I define a millimeter approach versus an all-out I-am-going-for-it or I-am-going-for-broke attitude.

In this book, I am going to go against mainstream gurus who talk about taking massive action and big leaps to get you where you want to go. The reality is that few people actually ever take this approach. Why? I believe there are two major reasons. The first one is fear: fear of failure, fear of change, fear of not accomplishing what you set out to do, fear of ridicule, fear of what your friends and family will say, and fear of not being good enough to succeed.

The second reason and one that is probably not as obvious is that most people inherently want to take an easier path or approach to success. Let me explain. Everyone wants to have success whether it is personal, business or professional, and they set goals to achieve these successes. However, most people would rather take the easiest road possible and expend the least amount of energy to get to these goals. (I know for some of you reading this, you might be thinking I am not very motivating.)

Let's talk reality for a moment and not sugarcoat it. Big leaps toward any goal can seem monumental and difficult, and can discourage you from even trying. But what if there was a way you could succeed at X, Y or Z in easy bite-size pieces that seemed manageable? And instead of trying to make huge changes in your lifestyle, business or professional life, you could instead make smaller "millimeter" changes and still achieve your goals. Would you like to know more? Well, this book is for you, because this is exactly what I am going to share and propose you do.

The "millimeter" approach to achieving your goals can be done a millimeter at a time. Just let me show you how it's done!

Donna

Dr. Donna Galante

PART 1
IT'S ALL ABOUT MILLIMETERS AND YOUR BUSINESS

CHAPTER 1:
WHAT IS THE "MILLIMETER" APPROACH TO BUSINESS AND LIFE?

"Your life does not get better by chance, it gets better by change."
— *Jim Rohn*

Let's start with the basic definition of a millimeter, which according to the dictionary is a unit of length equal to one thousandth of a meter and equivalent to 0.03937 inch. In other words, it is a very small amount. In my world, which happens to be as a practicing orthodontist for over 26 years, it is what we measure every day on every patient.

It determines our success in correcting a bite problem or properly positioning formerly crooked teeth. We measure the patients' initial problems in millimeters. For example, we measure the amount of an overbite in millimeters. Too much and it needs correction or none at all is also a big problem from an orthodontic standpoint.

We measure the amount of crowding in a patient's mouth in millimeters. It will help us determine if we can solve the problem with just braces, or we may need to place other appliances to expand or even maybe remove some teeth to make room. Your family dentist also is using "millimeters" to measure results. A crown that is placed on a tooth needs so many millimeters of coverage around the base of the tooth for an excellent, tight fit. Dental implants, very popular right now, need so many millimeters of clearance between the teeth for ideal placement and an excellent result.

When you go to the dentist and get your teeth cleaned, you may have had the pockets around your teeth measured in millimeters. You may have heard numbers ranging from one to four or even higher. These numbers are all in millimeters and indicate the health or possible diseased areas of your mouth.

A MILLIMETER MARATHON

Okay, that is it for the dental lecture. I just wanted to prove my point that for a very long time myself and others like me in the dental profession measure everything using millimeters. I started to realize that I was taking my millimeter approach to treating my patients and using the same type of measurements in other areas of my life. Let me share with you a story that will illustrate my approach to using millimeters to achieve your goals.

I started running in high school on the track and field team. I wasn't very good, but it was still fun to be part of a team and surround myself with some exceptional runners. When I entered college in 1976, I decided that I was not much of a sprinter and started to run cross-country. Thus, my love of long-distance running started to unfold. By the time I entered dental school, I was running up to 10 miles a day several times a week. I entered several races, 10K and half marathons, but always had the goal to complete a full marathon.

Fast forward through orthodontic school, marriage, the build of my practice, and two children, and I was now only running the occasional three miles maybe three times a week. Of course, I had my new year's resolution each year to run that marathon before I turned 50. May 2007, I was at our local dental society monthly dinner meeting. We meet once a month for a nice dinner, to hear a guest speaker, and do some great networking with colleagues.

This particular evening, one of my fellow orthodontic colleagues, announced that he was planning to run the California International Marathon in December 2007. This was the 25th anniversary of this particular race, and he wanted fellow dentists to join him. We were asked to get pledges and raise money for our local Smiles For Kids Charity. Each year our local Sacramento Dental Society raises money to provide needed dental care and orthodontics for children. Most of the treatment is provided pro-bono, but the money raised helps with supplies that are needed to treat these children. My colleague knew I was a runner and basically volunteered for me to do the marathon with him. (He called out my name in front of 400 of my fellow dentists... what could I say other than yes?)

So now I professed to 400 people that I was going to run 26.2 miles on December 2, 2007. I sat down and realized that maybe I should have left before the dessert.

Have you ever made a goal and not only had it written down, but also shared it with someone? How about sharing it with 400 people? Well, you can understand that I was now going to run this marathon no matter what. The next day I decided I needed to get a plan in place so that I would run the race and not be carried away in a stretcher. I called a friend who I knew ran marathons all the time — and he suggested a running group.

I asked for a second option as I knew with my schedule a running group would not work since I still had three offices to manage, two children and a husband. I needed a more flexible training schedule. He suggested purchasing the book *First Time Marathoner* by Jeff Galloway. His advice was to follow the program in the book for the first-time marathoner and I would be successful. I purchased the book later that day. The book became my coach. (10 years of college, dental school and orthodontic school train you well for reading books and using the library).

The good news was that I was able to jump ahead a few weeks because I could already run three miles. If you are reading this and you have run a marathon, there are lots of ways to train for it and I am not an expert. I am just sharing how I did it — it is a great model for the millimeter approach. The training basically involved running about three times a week and adding on mileage only on the weekend run. Each Saturday or Sunday you would add a mile to your run. During the week when you were not running, you could swim, bike, do yoga or just rest. It was the perfect training program for me.

Each week I would add a mile to my long run. Eventually I was running 13 miles, enough to enter a half marathon, which I did in October of that year. It was a great event — I felt terrific. I also accomplished my goal under my estimated time. I continued to add mileage each weekend until finally I ran 22 miles about three weeks before the actual marathon. Honestly, he (the book's author) wanted me to run an entire marathon of 26.2 miles, but I was not going to do that unless there was a medal and a massage in it for me.

So the millimeter approach (or mile by mile) required that I added on the mileage and went from barely running three miles in May 2007 to 22 miles in November 2007 three weeks before the big event. I felt confident I could go the entire 26.2 miles without a problem. The day of the marathon was cold in Sacramento. We were told to wear warm clothes that we could shed on the sidewalk as we ran. They would pick up the discarded clothing and donate the sweat pants and shirts later.

I was excited, but nervous to go for it. I had pledges in place for Smiles For Kids and now I just needed to prove that I could do it. In the training process I was taught to run then walk. My initial run/walk cycle was six minutes of running to one minute of walking. By the time I reached the 13.2-mile marker, I was at eight minutes of running to one minute of walking and feeling great. The weather was cold and windy the entire morning, so the only clothes I ended up shedding were my gloves. I did not initially wear heavy sweat pants and shirts. I took the layered approach. At mile marker 18, my family was there to greet me and take video of me running. Mile 18 is often called "The Wall" where people stop and get picked up in the vans. I was still feeling great. There were people giving up even before the mile marker eight.

There was this voice in my head that said, "Donna, come on! You're 49 years old and running a marathon. Are you kidding? You can't possibly finish this race without getting hurt. Look at all these people younger than you who are calling it quits and going home and getting a massage. That is what you need, a massage and then a nice Cabernet."

It went something like that, over an over in my head as I watched people "bail" out of the marathon. Some of them just walked away and others limped off the street. I tried not to pay attention to what was happening around me. There were the occasional water stops and some snacks they were giving out along the way. The best motivator was the people cheering you on from the sidelines. That really helped me stay focused and motivated. I also had my iPhone, which was playing music, and my husband could call me and speak to me as I was running.

So I passed mile marker 18 (aka "The Wall") without a problem. My family was there to cheer me on — and I was actually videotaped smiling and waving to them. By the time I reached mile 22, the people running around me had thinned out considerably. There was an ambulance right after the 22-mile marker. I decided not to look at what was happening. The voice in my head that was negative had now become a whisper, because I was only four miles away from my goal of finishing this race. I knew in my heart and soul I had trained well and did the needed work to succeed. Now it was just my willingness to persist and finish the race.

As I approached mile marker 23, I decided I was going to run as fast I as could for the last three miles. No more stopping to walk. I felt great and my legs were ready for the challenge. The last 3.2 miles I ran, not jogged over the finish line and completed my first marathon in four hours, 36 minutes and some change in seconds. I was elated as my goal was to finish in less than five hours!

There is more: My millimeter approach to training not only allowed me to finish the marathon in less time than my goal, I also felt so good that after I went home and took an ice bath (not too fun but necessary) and a shower, I spent the next three hours shopping for Christmas gifts with my daughter.

Have you ever accomplished a really big goal? How did you feel?

I think there was a tremendous amount of adrenaline running through my body that day. I can say I felt like I was "walking on clouds." It was a tremendous feeling of accomplishment and empowerment. Empowerment, which is what achieving our goals gives us. It empowers us to do more, make a difference, and live the lives we have dreamed about living.

ACHIEVE YOUR DREAMS IN MILLIMETERS

If you are reading this book and feel like you have given up on your dreams, your goals to achieve more, do more, and be more, I am here to tell you, you can still achieve all you desire. Apply the principle of millimeters to whatever it is that you have set to do now or in the past. It is never too late. I ran a marathon four months before my 50th birthday. It was a goal I had since I was 25.

How many goals, dreams or desires have you given up on? You don't have to give up.

The millimeter approach is a way to get it done by making the small changes consistently and with a definite plan in place. The millimeter approach is the path to achieving your big goals by breaking them down into bite-size pieces — tasks that you can accomplish readily and not based on your current situation. So dig up your goals and start breaking them down into millimeter segments. Your goals and dreams can be huge, but getting there does not need to be.

This book will help you use the millimeter approach to plan out a strategy to achieve your goals. There are stories of successful individuals who have used a millimeter approach to accomplish their goals in business, professionally and personally. With small changes and small steps, the "millimeter approach" can make a big impact on your life, your business, your family, your future and your happiness.

CHAPTER 2:
WHY MILLIMETERS MATTER SO MUCH IN YOUR BUSINESS

"You must do the thing you think you cannot do."
— Eleanor Roosevelt

I am writing this book during one of the worst economic declines since the Great Depression. People have called it the "Great Recession." However you name it, it has taken a huge toll on small businesses as well as professional practices. As an orthodontist practicing for over 26 years, I can say without a doubt, it has been one of the most challenging times in our practices. I have been through several recessions since I started practicing in 1986, but none of those previous economic declines lasted this long and did not have the permanent changes that are occurring in the economy now.

In the past, it was unheard of that a dentist or any specialist would close their offices at the end of the day, declare bankruptcy, and never come back. But that is exactly what is happening in my local community in Northern California and across other states that were significantly impacted by the massive downturn in the economy. Businesses around our orthodontic practice also were closing down, and no new businesses were coming in to replace them.

Commercial real estate in our area has a vacancy rate of 50 percent. A major retailer, Mervyn's, in the shopping center next to us went out of business. There were a multitude of restaurants and other businesses that closed, and the spaces they occupied remained empty. The housing market was a huge part of our local economy and when foreclosures started to occur, the contractors, builders, electricians, painters, plumbers, furniture stores and all the other businesses that provide products and services for homeowners, dried up overnight.

There were, however, businesses and professional practices that not only survived, but also thrived during this time. How did they do it? I propose they used a millimeter approach, of course. For example, our own practice, which had been growing anywhere from 10-50 percent a year since 1997, for the first time had no growth in 2008 and declined 30 percent in 2009. We were in a "free-fall" and realized that this recession was here to stay.

We needed to take action and take it fast, but what action was needed?

Our practice had been growing consistently for over 10 years. In fact in late 2007, we moved our main practice to a brand new beautiful building. We needed the space as we had outgrown our current location. The area we moved into was promoted as the next "hot" area in our community — they touted there would be restaurants, movie theaters, shopping and more. By the time we moved in — and, of course invested over $1.5 million in the building and improvements needed for our practice — within a short six months, the phone had stopped ringing. The restaurants and movie theaters never materialized and the stores that did open were closed within a few months.

Many of our patients come from referrals from other general dentists. As their practices slowed down, our referrals disappeared. In the past, parents would easily purchase braces for their children. They often used home equity lines of credit, applied fast-and-easy credit cards, or cashed out stocks from a booming stock market. All of those methods of procuring payment evaporated overnight. Breadwinners lost their jobs, homes were foreclosed, and bankruptcies became commonplace. As other survival needs kicked into gear for the average household, many families decided that the investment in braces for parents or children needed to be put on hold.

THE WHAT?

What would be the millimeter approach for our practice? I am going to share with you that at first we did nothing. Yes, nothing, because we were in denial. Have you been there? Denial: you make excuses for your business or practice. We did and this is what it sounded like:

"It is tax time (April) and people are busy paying their taxes."

"It is the end of school and graduations are occurring. Parents are too busy right now!"

"It is the start of summer and everyone is on vacation. When they come back they will get their braces on."

You get the picture.

The denial stage lasted about four months. I realized that my excuses were not going to work anymore. There was a significant change in the economy, and it was not going to get any better anytime soon.

Then we went from denial to anger, which sounds like this:

"How did this happen?"

"How can this happen to us? We just built this beautiful new office and expanded. It isn't fair."

Next we quickly went from anger to victim mode, which sounds like this:

"It is not our fault the practice is declining."

"The economy is the problem. There is nothing we can do about it."

Eventually depression set in. When you have the victim mentality you feel like there is nothing you can do about the situation. You are stuck, and there is no way out. You decide to hunker down and adopt a survival mentality. You figure, eventually the recession will go away. It always does. Meanwhile you start the cutbacks. You reduce the hours the practice is open; you eliminate marketing, reduce supply costs, and the worst thing you can do — lower fees.

BEEN THERE, DONE THAT, CHANGE THAT!

We did it all. And guess what, it helped, but we were still sinking faster than the Titanic. The measures we took helped with cash flow, but we were still missing out on our core business. Patients needing and wanting orthodontic treatment were still at the cornerstone of our practice growth and success. We needed to do something. We needed a millimeter approach.

What was our millimeter approach?

As a business practicing the millimeter approach, we took a close look at all aspects of our practice and discovered more about what went wrong. Once we uncovered all the challenges we faced, we developed an overall strategy that we felt would bring our practice back to health. Besides the economic turmoil that had occurred, there were three other factors that were responsible for our practice decline. Those factors were: competition, profitability and customer service (aka patient experience).

Competition in our area had grown substantially from about six orthodontists to over 28 in a six-mile radius from our main practice location. The population had increased some, but not nearly enough to support or warrant that many practices. Fees were lowered as the competition for the patients who needed braces increased. It became common to see fees that we were charging 15 or 20 years ago. There were more and more patients coming in to our office seeking multiple quotes. For example, we had one family who had been to 10 orthodontists in their quest to make sure they had been given the lowest fee.

The issue of practice profitability was another piece of the puzzle. As we had grown so rapidly and expanded, our gross revenue had increased tremendously, but our profit margin had declined. We were working harder, but not making more money that we could put into our bank account. Staffing costs had gone up along with everything else. We were spending money recklessly, which is not the way a millimeter practice would operate.

Finally, we discovered that our patient experience in our offices had declined. Some patients complained about the wait time to be seen for scheduled appointments. Furthermore, patients were upset with the perceived lack of appointment availability. As the economy continued to falter, working parents felt nervous about taking time off from work to bring themselves or even their children to appointments. We had developed a schedule that was good for us, but not really our patients and their parents.

THE MILLIMETERS TAKEN

Once we had all the factors uncovered, a plan was formulated using a millimeter approach.

First, we realized the economy was here to stay, and we needed to make some changes in our fees and how patients paid us. At first, we took the wrong approach and lowered fees to compete with all the other practices that offered discounted treatment. This policy eventually ends up with practices bankrupt due to competing with each other for the lowest fee around. We quickly got out of that game.

We realized that our fees did not need to be reduced to bargain-basement prices. Instead, we needed to offer our families a way to make their monthly payments lower. In orthodontics, most offices will extend interest-free payments over the course of the treatment. Instead of lowering fees, we would extend the payments out further, beyond the treatment time to make it affordable for our families.

This millimeter approach, a small change in our financial policy, produced a massive result in the number of patients now getting started in treatment because of affordable monthly payments. The risk to our practice was that the patients would stop paying as soon as their braces came off. This situation rarely happened as we implemented another strategy to make sure payments were received on a timely basis. How? We used an auto-draft system, which took payments right out of our patients' bank accounts or drafted credit card charges each on a patient-chosen date. This auto-draft kept our past-due accounts down to less than one percent uncollected. Another millimeter change with big rewards financially.

Because of the competition for patients seeking braces, we decided it was time to niche ourselves. We looked around and saw that most practices were not offering Invisalign to their patients. Invisalign provides a solution to obtain straight teeth without wearing braces. We saw an opportunity to provide that service and niche ourselves as the Invisalign orthodontic office.

The addition of a new type of braces was well received, and we discovered that patients, especially adults, who had for years wanted straight teeth but did not want to wear braces, were coming in and getting orthodontic treatment. By positioning ourselves in the Invisalign market niche, we were able to gain many more adult patients who never would obtain orthodontic treatment because they did not want to wear braces. Using the millimeter approach, we changed our marketing messages in all the media we used. A small change in our message brought about huge returns in the number of patients who came to seek our services. By becoming "the Invisalign orthodontist," we were able to capture a new pool of patients who would not otherwise have had treatment.

Using a millimeter approach, we were also able to uncover a specific type of orthodontic treatment that most other practices had ignored. Our focus on Invisalign as our orthodontic appliance of choice for our patients enabled our practice to grow over 60 percent from 2009 through 2012. During the same time period, nationwide statistics showed a 47 percent decrease in orthodontic practice revenue.

A question that comes up often is: How did you decide to niche yourselves using Invisalign as the brand of braces you would primarily offer?

We used a millimeter approach, of course.

There are many different types of braces on the market. The most common are the ones that go on the front of the teeth. The silver ones you see most often have been around since the 1900s. They have changed in size — and these types of braces are even now available in ceramic or clear. They are what we call in this business the "workhorse" in orthodontics. There are also braces that go behind the teeth. They have been around a long time as well. They are a popular option for those on TV or in the public eye. You would never know a person is wearing them — they are hidden on the back of the teeth. Finally, there are removable braces (aka Invisalign). They are clear, removable aligners that gradually straighten your teeth. They are a relatively new technology (1999) and provide the opportunity for adults in particular to gain healthy and beautiful smiles without the discomfort or appearance of traditional braces.

We looked at Invisalign closely as a niche for us because they were spending millions of dollars in marketing, in print and on television. We certainly did not have millions to spend on marketing. Invisalign also had a product that adults were interested in. We knew that many adults wanted straight teeth, but would not get braces. Invisalign provided a solution for them. Finally, we found data that indicated improved practice profitability and efficiency with Invisalign. Our goals included a more profitable practice along with better efficiency.

Improving our patients' experiences was another key factor in our decision to niche ourselves as an Invisalign practice. We discovered that patients did not need to be seen quite as often and that we had less emergency visits. This shift enabled us to provide appointments for our patients to suite their needs.

What will be your millimeter approach?

FACTORS AND CONSIDERATIONS TO APPLY

As you use the millimeter approach you will want to consider the following: 1) recognition of the real problem (no denial or any of the above); 2) do not make more excuses but instead take action; 3) move forward and do your homework or research on your market; 4) look for ways to improve, make efficient, and increase profitability in your business; 5) get creative and consistent in your customer service (doesn't matter what your business, customer service is always a high priority); and 6) make sure your services or products are beyond compare.

In our business, here is how all of those factors or considerations rolled out:

Number one, we recognized we had a problem that was not temporary, seasonal or just a fluke. It was here to stay, and we needed to quickly get a plan in place.

Millimeter businesses stop making excuses, realize the problem, and quickly take action.

Number two, we did our research — we knew the statistics about the number of adults who were candidates for orthodontic treatment versus the number who actually obtained treatment. The gap was related to lack of a choice of appliance. We recognized that Invisalign was the solution and committed to a new brand for our practice.

Millimeter businesses find, examine and fill the open holes in their marketplaces. Sometimes these holes are millimeters wide, but often more like kilometers wide. Millimeter businesses tap into those new markets as part of their re-branding strategies.

Number three, we wanted not only to niche ourselves, but also to become more profitable and efficient. We discovered through our research that Invisalign had a track record of providing more net income per patient and more efficiency in the dental office. Millimeter businesses want more net income and more efficiency in their operations.

Number four, we wanted to provide our patients with an exceptional experience. We wanted them to tell their friends and family about their amazing experiences in our practice. Invisalign helped us change our schedule to accommodate our patients and their schedules. Less visits, less time in the chair, and virtually no emergency visits, made our patients very happy.

Millimeter businesses are constantly looking at ways to improve customer service. Little millimeter changes can make a big difference in how your customers perceive the service they have received in your office or place of business. Our patients were much happier spending less of their valuable time in our dental chairs.

Finally, we wanted to make sure we were always at the cutting edge in providing the best service and products available to our patients. Invisalign was the newest technology available to help patients get their teeth and bites, healthy and beautiful. We spent and continue to spend hours in continuing education to perfect our technical experience with the appliance.

Millimeter businesses are those that constantly work to improve their products and service. They are constantly bringing new technology into their business to provide customers exceptional experiences. They are constantly educating themselves and their teams on these new technologies.

IN SUMMARY, A MILLIMETER APPROACH INVOLVES FIVE MAIN ACTIVITIES:

1. Recognition of a problem within their businesses, whether it is product-related or service-related. Those millimeter businesses take responsibility for the problem and get into action quickly.
2. Millimeter businesses dig deep to get answers in an effort to learn where the holes exist in their marketplaces and identify a way to target that potentially untapped market with millimeter precision.
3. These businesses strive for more net income and more efficiency. Millimeter businesses work smarter not harder.

4. They create exceptional customer service. They establish an amazing experience for customers, clients and patients, which is a millimeter business goal. A millimeter business looks at the small things that can be done to produce exceptional customer experiences and create raving fans.
5. They produce extraordinary products and services. They provide cutting-edge products, technology or services, which is another millimeter business goal. They look at other competitors in their industries and see what they are doing, and identify which competitor is having success. By spending time educating themselves and their teams, they can provide the best available products and services to their customer base.

As you read through this book you will learn how businesses and individuals have used this "millimeter" approach to achieve their goals and create success.

CHAPTER 3:
USING MILLIMETERS IN YOUR HIRING PROCESS

"You're braver then you believe, and stronger than you seem, and smarter than you think."
— A.A. Milne

The millimeter approach to hiring can bring your organization or business a new way to hire or recruit extraordinary personnel. Most small businesses can achieve more success and prosperity by using a millimeter approach to their hiring process. The success of your business or professional practice is dependant on having an extraordinary team in place.

Using a millimeter approach to hiring will help your business or professional practice thrive, no matter what the current economic conditions may be. You are taking small, well-thought-out steps to find extraordinary employees.

So what is this approach and how can you use it to attract, recruit, hire and retain millimeter employees? I am going to share with you seven steps we use in our practices to hire not just any employees, but those employees who are committed, engaged and extraordinary. When you approach your hiring process with a "millimeter" attitude, you hire people who will help your business and practice grow.

The first step is to make sure you are hiring to satisfy a real need in your business or professional practice.

From my personal experience, we often hired new people to fill a position that we felt needed a full-time employee. Looking back at those situations, we could have utilized our current team much more effectively and divided up the particular job among several employees. At first it may seem like the employee was getting "more work." While that might have been true, we often added a pay raise to compensate for the additional workload.

The added responsibilities were now met with a more positive attitude. It became more cost effective for us to give our current employees a pay raise than bring on new employees that would require time to train and of course additional payroll. If you hire right from the start, you will have employees who welcome new challenges and responsibilities.

Think carefully about what position is really needed in your business or practice and if there are other employees that can be moved into the vacant position. Hiring a new employee is a huge responsibility and one that should not be taken too lightly or decided too quickly.

The second step is to make sure you have clearly defined job descriptions.

Job descriptions are a detailed document that includes both what an employee is expected to do and the specific behaviors necessary to accomplish those tasks. It helps the potential employees know from day one what you, the employer, expect from them if they should be offered the position.

In our offices, we initially did not have clearly defined job descriptions written down. We simply had our key employees write down exactly what they do each and every day, week or month at our practice. From this list, we formulated an official job description.

To get a list of the personality traits required, we essentially looked at our top employees who were performing at the highest levels and wrote down their behaviors, attitudes and personalities. These became part of the job descriptions.

The third step is to recruit exceptional employees.

This process is typically the hardest depending on the size and type of business you own or manage. If you are like me, the owner of a professional practice, you will typically place an ad online or in a local newspaper. I am going to give you some other ideas and tactics that will give you some great opportunities to recruit extraordinary employees.

Possible Candidate Sources:
1. Networking with fellow business owners or professionals.
2. Employee Referrals. Give your employees an incentive to refer their circle of influence to your business or practice.
3. Customers, clients or patients. Let them know you are hiring. You can do this with email, online social media, a letter or even a simple flyer.
4. Social Media. Facebook in particular is a great way to get the word out that you are hiring. I had a long-term employee post on her Facebook that we were hiring for a scheduling coordinator and she handed me several resumes from her circle of influence. We ended

up hiring one of her "Facebook" friends. Because she is an employee that we respect and know is "invested" in the practice, we knew that we had the potential to hire another exceptional employee.
5. Focused advertising. You can place strategic ads in publications that are suited to your industry.
6. Email. We will often email our patients/parents and let them know of a possible job opening in our offices.
7. Your website is a good way to have an ongoing source of leads. You can add a contact form so that potential employees can submit their resumes.
8. Industry-specific headhunters and employment agencies.
9. Schools. In the dental field there are many vocational schools that are looking for externships for their students. These are great opportunities to "try" a potential employee out before giving them a full-time position.

The fourth step is to screen potential candidates via their resumes.

A business or professional practice that takes a millimeter approach to hiring will take the time to carefully review resumes and look at the details of employment that are presented. A millimeter approach will take into consideration job history, education, skills and references listed.

The fifth step to successful hiring is the interview process.

A millimeter approach to hiring takes into consideration the importance of the interview, both in person and over the phone.

In our practices, we developed a system for interviewing potential candidates over the phone first. This was usually delegated to an employee in a management position. Once the phone interview was conducted, the best candidates were given the opportunity to meet in person and be interviewed.

The sixth step to successful hiring is having specific and targeted questions for the interview.

In our practices, we developed lists of questions that would help us determine not only the skill level of potential employees, but also their behaviors and attitudes in certain situations.

These questions allowed us to understand how the potential employees would react in certain situations in our practice. They were key to understanding their behavior especially in stressful or confrontational situations. If they were able to effectively answer these questions that focused more on their behaviors or reactions to a situation (rather than their skills), they were more likely to get the job.

The seventh and final step in our approach to hiring was to make sure we had a training program in place for new hires.

The training program should be set up within a specific timeframe often two weeks to as long as 90 days or more where the new hire has to achieve a certain level of competence in a skill or knowledge that is essential to your business.

In our practices we have a 90-day training program in place with certain skills and acquired knowledge that is measured and tested on a weekly or monthly basis, which depends on the position. We regularly test the new employee, and if there is an issue we will discover early on what areas they may need additional help. If you look closely at each step of their training, you will be able to provide more focused training in areas that they are having a difficult time. Operating as a millimeter business, you will look at the small things that they are struggling with, or you will make the needed small changes in their training to get your desired results. Remember, it is the small changes or the little things that make the biggest difference.

Also, small changes either in your training process or in the new hire's specific area of responsibility are much easier to implement than a total overhaul of your entire process. Plus, spending a little bit more time with a new hire, someone who seems to be struggling with some of the skills and knowledge you want them to acquire and excel in, will in the long run be a good investment for your business.

From personal experience, whenever we deviated from the training program, we ended up having an employee who was good, but never great or even extraordinary. You know those types of personnel; they never do anything really wrong, but then again, they never really shine. Think about this in your business or in the businesses that you frequent. Wouldn't you agree there is an epidemic of mediocrity? What would happen to your business if you took a millimeter approach to your hiring?

CASE STUDY

Bill Burnett, Partner
Tailwind Discovery Group

We found that aside from evaluating the necessary skills needed for a job, the single most important thing we wanted from prospective employees was passion. Of course, passion will just translate into frustration if you don't have good leadership of the employee after he or she is hired.

On the skills side, we had one terrific technique for hiring analysts. In fact, we just used the technique with a group of executives to demonstrate its effectiveness. We give applicants a simple logic puzzle to solve. This puzzle can be solved within a few minutes by using trial and error. But what we require is that they also solve the puzzle without using trial and error. They have to demonstrate a solution with what the CIA calls a logical analytic line. We give them 24 hours to do so. The reason we give them that long is two-fold.

First, psychologists have now shown that we use what's called System One in our brains to quickly solve problems. System Two is where we do our purposeful deep thinking. Good analysts do not like to use System One even when it provides the quick and useable answer.

Second, the puzzle type we use has four different ways the puzzle can be solved, that is, four different analytic lines.

A great analyst will typically solve it with one line, then will see a hint in that line of another approach and they will pursue that as well, and so on. We often get three different analytic lines from good analysts. What is remarkable is how creative (and amusing) non-analytic thinking types can be in coming up with explanations after they've solved the puzzle using trial and error.

Hiring managers, of course, hire the person they like the most. We have had hiring managers ignore the outcome of this method and hire someone who did not demonstrate the ability to solve this puzzle with logic. Every time, this person failed in their analytic assignments. Everyone we hired who did solve the puzzle, turned out to be great employees. ■

IMPLEMENTING A "MILLIMETER APPROACH" IN YOUR HIRING PROCESS

1. Are there small millimeter-type changes needed in your hiring process? If so, what would some of these changes look like?
2. Can you list several changes in your new hire training that you can implement in the next 30 days? What impact would these changes have in your business or professional practice?
3. Do you have employees currently in job positions that are doing their job "okay", but not in an "extraordinary way"? If so, what can you do today to make a small but significant change in that employee's performance?

CHAPTER 4:
MILLIMETER BUSINESSES FOCUS ON THE "THREE Ts"

"Nothing diminishes anxiety faster than action."
— Walter Anderson

In the last chapter, we talked about recruiting and hiring new employees with a millimeter approach. Many businesses stop here when it comes to training. As recommended, the first few months of the new employees' tenure should include (in the millimeter approach) training and testing. There are procedures to learn, systems to understand, a culture to integrate into, plenty of new people to meet, and new friendships to form.

Once the employee passes through the initial training phase that may last two weeks to 90 days or even more, they are (in my opinion) then an official part of the team. You as their employer place them into their positions with the expectation that they will perform their duties with 100-percent accuracy and excellence.

Now I describe this as a best-case scenario in the perfect office environment. Unfortunately, this situation is not always the case. The average employee typically has had only bare minimum training required to perform his or her job — and if there was training involved it might have risen only to the level of mediocrity. Because of my experience in the dental field, I can say that for the majority of practices, minimal to zero ongoing training occurs with their teams. Outside of the dental field, many small business owners that I have spoken with share similar experiences in their businesses. Why does this happen? It's not because business owners and professional practices do not want well-trained staff. Of course they do; but it takes time and money, both of which can be in short supply in a small business and professional practice.

To get to the next level of excellence and extraordinary performance will require more training and testing of not only new hires, but also of current employees as well. As a millimeter business, you will be committed to what I call the Three Ts — train, train again and train some more.

MILLIMETER PRECISION AND ATTITUDE

When you hire new employees, a training program must be in place to consistently, efficiently and effectively impart the necessary skills and knowledge needed to perform their jobs with millimeter precision and a millimeter attitude.

So what are millimeter precision and millimeter attitude?

Just like a tooth that needs 1 mm more movement (remember from chapter 1), millimeter precision and attitude requires your new employee to master small things that result in extraordinary results. Part of this approach involves superior customer service, such as excellent product or service delivery. When I say this, I mean the company offers a product or service that has no competition or compare — it stands in a class all by itself. It is possible for any company to create this high standard when a focus on millimeters is put in place.

Now you may be asking, "I have a training program in place for new employees, but I don't understand why I need to continue to train and train again especially if their jobs stay the same?"

I used to feel the same way about training employees. I thought that once you trained them to perform specific duties, they would continue to do their jobs and actually get better at it over time. While I found that was true with about 20 percent of my employees, the vast majority constantly needed to be reminded of specific tasks or knowledge that they had previously learned. This would happen with employees who went through the initial training with no problems and even exceeded expectations. However, as they got more relaxed in their jobs and became further integrated into the practice, I discovered that they often forgot certain procedures, or their skills started to decline or become sloppy and inconsistent.

We gradually implemented training workshops as part of our monthly staff meetings. These workshops essentially reviewed procedures, protocols and scripts we use as part of our overall patient care. This also gave us the opportunity to look at what we were doing and make some millimeter-type changes to maximize their effectiveness in their jobs.

By training and training again, we developed employees with millimeter precision and attitude. These employees now on a regular basis rotate as leaders of our morning meetings each day before we start seeing patients. They look at procedures and systems and make recommendations for improvement and refinement. Since they have already been focused on millimeters of improvement with our patients' orthodontic results, they now take that approach with all aspects of patient care.

FINAL STEP: CONTINUOUS TRAINING

So now you have employees who are trained from the beginning, and you are consistently training and retraining them on your procedures and systems. The final step in this process is to continue to train them even more by adding more procedures, newer systems and advanced strategies.

Am I talking about making significant changes here? Yes, you got that right. Change, is always met with overall anxiety and sometimes downright hostility in most businesses. However, employees who have been trained with a millimeter attitude look at change differently. When your employees are constantly involved in the systems of your business through regular training, they will offer their suggestions to improve any aspect of your business. This has the benefit of improving their jobs and increasing your bottom line.

The employee who has been trained initially, trained again, and trained even more to look at the millimeters of his or her job, will become an employee dedicated to excellence. By investing in your employees' accomplishments in their jobs, they know you are an employer who is interested in helping them succeed. Furthermore, you will have employees aware of ways to improve your business through their trained millimeter lenses.

As a business owner, you cannot possibly know when all the moving parts of your business are not working at their maximum levels. When you have employees who have the millimeter attitude, they will always be on the lookout for millimeter ways to improve.

CASE STUDY

Halley Bock, CEO and president
Fierce, Inc., www.fierceinc.com

For Crate & Barrel, the "Fierce Conversations" training program was implemented with store managers across the country. The goal was to reinforce the company's culture of valuing good communication. Specifically, the "Fierce Conversations" training program helped Crate & Barrel create a culture where candor and curiosity are the expectation, developing great leaders — at all levels of the organization — by building practical, results-focused skills.

Through collaboration with Crate & Barrel executives, we determined the "Fierce Conversations" training curriculum would be most beneficial. "Fierce Conversations" aligns with Crate & Barrel's corporate culture, which values good communication. As Christy Lerner, regional trainer, southern region, said, "We've always talked about the right conversations and the right way to lead, so Fierce training really fits with what Crate believes; it resonates with our people and our culture."

"Fierce Conversations" is comprised of five modules:
- **The Foundation:** set the stage for change.
- **Team Conversations:** create internal think tanks and promote collaboration.
- **Coaching Conversations:** improve decision-making skills

and foster self-generated insight among all levels of the organization.
- **Delegation Conversations:** establish clear levels of decision-making and areas for growth.
- **Confrontation Conversations:** address attitudinal, behavioral or performance issues while enriching relationships.

By practicing these important business conversations, individuals walk away with easy-to-use tools to increase productivity, engagement and bottom-line success. Crate & Barrel was also looking for practical skills to engage staff and lead to appropriate employee development. "Fierce Conversations" offered concepts that were easy for the Crate & Barrel staff to remember and to implement. "Fierce is nothing like the theory-intensive programs that tend to confuse people and don't have much of a 'take back' for the job," said Christy.

All Fierce trainings are customized, because real conversations take place around the issues. In addition, Fierce training programs are designed for high levels of interactivity. Fierce uses "real playing" — not role playing — to train participants, allowing them to use real issues while learning the Fierce modules in virtual working sessions. Feedback from store managers was unanimously positive. Managers who participated in the Fierce training are able to quickly identify and resolve personnel issues with good communication skills, enabling staff to work more productively. They also learned how to "manage the right way," through open, honest communication and solid coaching skills that engage staff.

Training programs such as "Fierce Conversations," as well as Crate & Barrel's dedication to improving its employees' communication skills, has made the company an anomaly in the retail industry — a retailer associated with longevity and low turnover.

When considering training programs for employees, always start by holding them "able." Shift away from the mentality of holding others accountable. By holding each other "able," companies build a culture of engagement, trust and creativity versus disengagement, fear and disillusionment. When organizations hold their employees able, they choose to recognize the capacity each person has to achieve the goals. ∎

CASE STUDY

Misty Young
The Breakfast Lady

As we began to grow our small independent restaurant company, we realized the owners, who were normally "on deck," could no longer be the face to every single guest. We developed a comprehensive multimedia-training program to essentially replicate ourselves.

Included in our training program are totally custom manuals, job descriptions, checklists, quizzes, live-in-person training, and a series of completely custom training videos along with a comprehensive test. In addition to that we created a superstar hiring program, and a pre-working live audition training program that let us see what a prospective associate has before we put them out on the floor with our valued guests.

In addition, we created a comprehensive training program for our managers including structured reading and required timely book reports with bonuses, incentives for earning an iPad, off-site retreats with guest speakers and a structured program, role-playing and satisfaction surveys along with checklists and other tools that have proven beneficial to the managers and us, the owners in developing the company. Yes, we're a small company. We are family-owned (myself, my husband, our daughter, and our son-in-law), and we're considered a mom-and-pop business, but that doesn't mean we can't start acting as strategic as Apple behind the scenes. Since we rolled out the training program, we have seen less turnover, higher satisfaction, and we have grown from one restaurant location to four. Yes, in this economy — and that means the results we have seen have been increased guest happiness, increased revenues, and additional locations from which to serve. We are always looking at our training program and how we might modify it for continued success. ■

IMPLEMENTING THE "THREE T's" IN YOUR BUSINESS OR PROFESSIONAL PRACTICE:

1. What are you currently doing in your business or professional practice as far as ongoing training for your employees?
2. What small millimeter changes can you implement immediately to either enhance your current training program or begin the process of creating one?
3. Write down the steps and resources you will need to implement these changes in your training systems and the benefits you expect for your business and professional practice.

CHAPTER 5:
A MILLIMETER APPROACH TO YOUR SYSTEMS AND PROCEDURES

"The best thing you can do is the right thing; the next best thing you can do is the wrong thing; the worst thing you can do is nothing."
— *Theodore Roosevelt*

When I first started my own practice in 1988, I had zero systems in place. Not only did I lack any real systems, I didn't even know exactly what they were for or why I needed them. Fortunately, I read Michael Gerber's book, *The E-Myth,* shortly after I had opened my office. It probably took me another two to three years to figure out what systems I needed, get them in place, and make sure my staff was trained in those systems.

In the meantime, like the business owner in Gerber's book, I had a business that owned me morning, noon and night and I quickly became burnt out, worn out and depressed over my situation. My education up to this point in my life had been mostly geared toward getting into a competitive dental school. I had never taken a single business, accounting or economics class, and definitely not one on marketing. We were told in dental school that if you were a great dentist, you could hang your "shingle" anywhere and you would be successful.

That might have been true in the '60s, '70s and first part of the '80s, but as I found out, it was not true in the late '80s and even more so now. You need to be not only a great doctor, but to be truly successful in practice today you need to know how to manage, market, lead and implement. You could be the best implant dentist in the world, but unless you have a system in place to generate new patients, diagnose their problems, and present them with treatment plans and financing options, you will have minimal success and patients will not seek your services.

My initial practice earned me an honorary MBA just by going through the process of learning not only what systems I needed to put into place, but also how to set them up and get them implemented on a consistent basis. The first two years of being in practice for myself almost took me down permanently and forced me to contemplate leaving the profession. Fortunately, I started to implement the needed systems and set up procedures that would ultimately turn the practice around to be profitable and eventually sellable.

From my personal experience, I have learned that taking a millimeter approach to setting up systems in your business is necessary from the beginning. What is the millimeter approach to setting up systems in your place of business? As a millimeter business, you are committed to taking responsibility for both your success and failure in your business. As you dig deeper to find the reason for your lackluster sales, low productivity of your team, or the general malaise in your business, you will understand that your lack of systems, clear policies and procedures could be causing your business not to perform.

A MILLIMETER APPROACH TO YOUR SYSTEMS AND PROCEDURES

A millimeter approach would be to immediately address the biggest challenge you are having and getting a plan in place to improve your systems. For example, we were having great success at getting patients into our offices for an initial consultation. Our marketing was working extremely well, but the number of patients who were accepting treatment was abysmal.

We started to look at the entire "new patient process" and take it apart a millimeter at a time. This enabled us to look at each contact that we had with the prospective patient. With a millimeter perspective, we looked at how we could enhance the new patient experience from the moment they called our office and scheduled their appointments, through the actual exam and consultation, and even continuing on with our follow-up process.

By taking a look at the entire process, we made small changes that were actually simple to implement and did not involve a large expense. Those small changes were measured and analyzed and if necessary changed slightly to make them even more effective. Our results were stunning. We went from 50 percent of the new patients consenting to treatment to a 91-percent acceptance rate in a period of about three months. Our data now is a full 24 months with this system in place, and even now we are averaging 88 percent acceptance even in this challenging economy.

Once we looked at the process with a millimeter focus, we uncovered many small ways we could improve our new patient process that ended up with a massive impact on our practice. We then made sure that our system for orchestrating the new patient process was solidified in our systems manual, so that any future and current employees would be trained in a consistent and successful way.

I am sure you are excited to know exactly what we did to make such a huge improvement and lucky for you I am going to share the details. The steps were as follows:

Step 1: Recognize the problems

Step 2: Make changes right from the beginning of your process

Step 3: Work smarter not harder

Step 4: Focus on customer service

Step 5: Emphasize learning and education

We first changed how we handled the initial phone call from the prospective patient. We used a script that followed along with a printed form that required my team to get a fairly significant amount of information regarding the prospective patient. Often the patients or parents were in a hurry to try to get the appointment scheduled in between their other 20 things on their to-do lists. While we like to gather as much information as possible, it was neither realistic nor customer-service oriented to keep them on the phone for 20 minutes gathering all the details. We shortened the information that we needed to the basics and could get all the data we needed and an appointment scheduled in five minutes. This made the prospective patient much happier and joyful right from the start. Next, we sent them a letter that confirmed the appointment and told them a little more about our office and doctors. We also included any brochures or information that would be helpful to their initial concerns.

We use automated email reminders of appointments, but also with our new patients, we have our scheduling manager personally call them a day or two before the appointment to make sure they know where the office is located, verify they have the right time and date, and let them know the doctor was looking forward to meeting them soon.

This simple gesture prevented patients from not showing up for their appointments.

Once they were in the office, they were immediately greeted by one of my team, taken on an office tour, and given a seat in our private exam room. Coffee, tea, water or lemonade is offered and some additional paperwork to fill out. We include a health history form, a questionnaire about their orthodontic concerns for themselves or their children, and information about what type of braces we have available, and what type they want. We also provide a form that shares some personal information about the doctors.

The form introduces the doctors and lists their favorite foods, movies, pets, and other information. We then ask the patient to fill in their favorite foods, movies, etc. This has been a great way to "break the ice," as most patients will list a pet, movie or food that the doctors can relate to and immediately get the patient comfortable with the entire process. The doctor comes in, performs the exam and consultation, and outlines a proposed treatment plan. We found that most patients will indicate on their forms what type of braces they prefer, so we just need to let them know that they are candidates for treatment, how long it will take, and what it costs.

We discovered that by keeping it simple, focusing on what they were concerned about and presenting solutions that addressed their concerns, it gave us more people willing to commit to treatment. Many of our new patients would share that they were going to get other opinions, talk with their spouses about the plan, or let us know they were not going to make a decision until after they were back from vacation. We encouraged them to do all that they needed to make the best decisions for their families. However, we made sure they left our office with several gifts and guarantees that we offer. Our child and teen patients would receive a special gift bag that contained chapstick, pens, pencils, hand sanitizer, mints, our practice newsletter, and additional referral cards.

The parents would receive a book that I had written called *Healthy and Beautiful at Any Age: Your Smile and Modern Orthodontics*. The book established me as an expert and increased my credibility with the patient and parents. The family that would come in with one child and bring in all their friends or siblings would also receive a special gift bag. You can visualize how that looked when they left the office and opened their bags with excitement as they walked through our reception areas. A handwritten note personally signed by the doctor would be immediately generated along with a summary report of our proposed treatment plan. Patients would often receive these in the mail the very next day. If the patient did not schedule an appointment to get started with their orthodontic treatment, a detailed and precise follow-up program was put into place. We would always ask the patient permission to contact them after they had a chance to get other opinions or discuss the treatment with a spouse. If we were unsuccessful with the phone call follow-up, we implemented a 90-day mailing campaign that would send them a series of six greeting cards, all very fun and personalized to their homes to let them know we were here to help when they were ready.

Finally, if they still were undecided, we then placed them into our database so that they would receive our printed newsletters and other correspondence so they would stay connected to our practice. Until the patient eventually scheduled to start orthodontic treatment in our office or let us know that they made other plans, they would continue to receive our correspondence.

As part of our follow-up system, twice a year, we would send them a fun letter (usually from one of our pets or children) inviting them to come back in and get their treatment started. Of course, there would be an offer with a deadline to respond. This alone would bring back patients that we had seen anywhere from one to six years ago.

As you can see, our process is systemized so that all our prospective patients receive the same communication and are given the same experience in the practice. Before we took a millimeter approach, we would see new patients, give them a treatment plan, send out summary letters (with no urgency), and basically make a few follow-up calls. If they did not respond, we would assume they did not want treatment.

When we looked at it from a millimeter perspective, we realized that we needed to operate like a millimeter business would.

First, we recognized that there was big problem and took responsibility. We did not blame the economy, our location or the competition. Second, we looked at the areas where we could make small changes, but have a big impact. We realized we had multiple areas that needed improvement. Most of the improvements that were needed, we were able to implement quickly and with minimal cost.

Third, we had the new patients coming in the door. Our marketing was working, but we were working too hard and not getting results. Millimeter businesses work smarter not harder. We were working hard to get the patients to come in the first place, but failing miserably at getting them to commit to treatment.

Fourth, we needed to make sure our new patients had a memorable and amazing experience in our office. Millimeter businesses are always looking at ways to improve their customers' (patient) experiences. Little things like a gift bag or a handwritten card take minimal expense and time, but provide a powerful message to the new patient.

The fifth and final goal of a millimeter business is to always be learning and educating themselves on how they can do or be better. The system you put into place today may need some small changes (millimeter changes) in a few months or years. We realize that as a millimeter practice, we are always measuring our results and looking for ways to improve. Systems, however, are the cornerstone of a successful millimeter business or practice. Without systems in place, your team and your business will not be able to operate with millimeter precision.

Measuring your success and results is hard to do when everyone is doing it differently. Your ability to get your systems in place and get your team trained on those systems will determine how quickly you achieve your goals. Millimeter businesses realize systems need to be evaluated and changed and are willing to do that on a regular basis. We needed to change our new patient process and develop a better system that brought us the results we were looking for.

In the next chapter, I will dive into how a marketing system needs to be organized, implemented, analyzed and changed with a millimeter approach.

IMPLEMENTING A "MILLIMETER APPROACH" TO YOUR BUSINESS OR PRACTICE SYSTEMS:

1. What system, procedure or policy in your business or professional practice needs to be redesigned?
2. What can you do immediately in a small, easy-to-implement way that will bring a big impact to your business or professional practice?
3. How can you, on a regular basis, take a millimeter approach to your systems, procedures and policies so that you are able to consistently and effectively make the needed changes to keep growing in your business or professional practice?

CHAPTER 6:
MARKETING WITH MILLIMETER PRECISION

*"It doesn't matter where you are,
you are nowhere compared to where you can go."*
— *Bob Proctor*

For most business owners, marketing is considered an afterthought or something that they have to do but would rather sleep on a bed of nails. I know the feeling — most of my professional career, I felt the same way. Marketing, though, is one of the most essential activities you can ever do to invest in and grow your business. If you are a business owner and you're not spending at least 50 percent of your time marketing or you have not hired someone to do your marketing then your business is not living up to its potential.

Most people don't realize the value and importance of marketing, because in the old economy you could get away with doing less of it and survive just fine. Mainstream experts didn't necessarily promote marketing either as a necessary part of doing business, and general beliefs of other business practitioners often perpetuated this mentality. For example, when I was in dental school and then again in my orthodontic residency, leaders in the field recommended that if I wanted to start a practice to just hang my sign and watch the flood of patients come through the door. Since I had never taken a single business or marketing course while in college or dental school, I figured the professors who were older and wiser and more successful than me knew the truth. The truth as I understood it was that if you have a DDS or DMD after your name, you could live wherever you wanted and with little effort have a booming practice by hanging up your diploma and a sign.

Guess what I found out?

It was not true!

My first practice that I opened in the Philadelphia suburbs almost did not happen. It was the late '80s and between my school-loan debt and an upcoming recession, the banks were not too excited about giving a single female with no history of credit a loan to start a practice. I was already working as an associate orthodontist in several different locations in Pennsylvania and New Jersey. As I proceeded down the path to opening my own practice, I discovered that banks were not willing to lend me the money.

I was shocked. They had lent me all the tens of thousands of dollars I needed to go through dental school and my orthodontic training. At that time the interest rates were at 18 percent as well. It wasn't until I had a conversation with a patient who knew a banker who was motivated to lend to new females in business that I received my loan for my start-up practice.

Of course I was excited, because I had no clue that I would not succeed. After all, I thought all I had to do was hang up my diploma and the patients would appear. As you probably have guessed by now that did not occur.

In fact the opposite occurred. My phone did not ring at all. It was a struggle to get new patients, and I ended up working several associate jobs just to make payments on my debt. I eventually did sell that practice and move to California and was able to pay off my bank loans with the proceeds from the sale of the practice. However, I still did not understand that my success in my practice was not tied to my diploma, but was all about marketing.

I think most small businesses struggle with the idea of marketing or promoting their business or as a professional, promoting themselves to the public. As a dentist, I felt that I did all the hard work in college, then dental school, and even more so in my orthodontic specialty training. I deserved to have patients call and make appointments. My diploma was all I needed.

Even when I relocated to California, I still did not fully understand that marketing was the only way patients were going to know about our office and the great service and results we provided. It took until 2008 when we went through a major economic crisis in our area, to realize that without a consistently implemented marketing plan in place that is measured with millimeter precision, a successful dental practice was just a "pipe" dream.

MARKETING WITH PRECISION

So what do businesses that market with millimeter precision look like? They all have the following characteristics:

A millimeter business will budget money toward marketing.

This is the first step that millimeter businesses take. They realize they need to spend money on marketing in order to make money. They also know how much money they are willing to spend to obtain the number of clients, customers or patients they are looking to obtain. They know that a customer, client or patient is worth on average X amount of dollars. With that number in place, they can put a certain amount of money toward marketing each month to achieve the number of customers, clients and patients they have set as a goal.

A millimeter business will have a marketing plan.

The first step is to set up a marketing plan. Most business owners never do this, and it is so simple. Millimeter businesses know that a marketing plan is essential to a successful and profitable business. Furthermore, they also know that a plan is a starting place. Marketing ideas, strategies and tactics need to be changed and updated as they are implemented. Millimeter businesses know that some strategies and tactics are going to work brilliantly and others will be a tremendous flop.

They are willing to implement and get their action plans in place and then decide if it was a success or not. They know that the majority of what they do will not work to their level of expectation. However, they also know that certain strategies and tactics will perform so well that those that underperform will not make a dent in their profits.

This takes us to the next characteristic of a millimeter business.

A millimeter business will have a marketing calendar.

In order for a millimeter business to successfully implement their marketing strategies and tactics, they know they need to write it down. Millimeter businesses will have a marketing calendar in place so that they never forget to implement their strategies and tactics at the right time and do so consistently.

Without a written calendar in place, a millimeter business may get so busy with other duties of business that they forget or push aside the most important aspect of their business or practice…marketing. A calendar will prevent certain strategies and tactics from not being implemented. Millimeter businesses will have a designated employee or assistant responsible for organizing and maintaining the calendar.

Millimeter businesses will meet with their marketing coordinator or designated employee weekly to get updates on what is happening that week, month or quarter. The designated employee, in a millimeter business, is excited and energized about the marketing the business or practice is doing. The marketing specialist brings the owner solid, implementable ideas.

A marketing calendar for a millimeter business is a simple but powerful strategy for successful marketing campaigns.

Millimeter businesses will measure and track all marketing they do.
When a millimeter business starts to develop a marketing plan and puts it into a calendar for implementation, they learn quickly to measure and track their results. They understand that their resources are limited and need to make sure that the money they are spending on a particular strategy or tactic will ultimately bring them the desired results.

Millimeter businesses will use tracking numbers on print ads, Internet ads and other media that requires a potential customer, client or patient to call for an appointment. These tracking numbers can then be directly linked to that media that was seen by the particular customer. Knowing how they found your business is an ideal way to monitor marketing efforts.

Millimeter businesses also have well-trained employees who are either answering the phone or greeting customers face to face. These employees trained in the millimeter way, will be able to connect, relate and communicate effectively with your potential customer, client or patient. Through their efforts, more information is gained regarding how the customer found your business, what their needs are, and how your business has a solution for their problem or need.

Millimeter businesses are constantly revising their marketing plan and calendar.

Most businesses will get a plan in place and decide that is all they needed to do. They did the hard work, now they have a plan, and they are going to use it forever. This is not the case with a millimeter business. A millimeter business knows that a marketing plan is in a constant state of flux. Because they are measuring the results on a regular basis, they know that there will be certain strategies and tactics that even with some changes will need to be eliminated and replaced with something different.

Millimeter businesses realize that marketing requires ongoing implementation, change and often-total elimination. These businesses that actively participate in revising their plan and calendar will find the most success.

The final characteristic of a millimeter business is that it is a constant student of marketing.

A millimeter business understands that education is key to success and profits in its business. Learning from others and attending seminars in person or online is a key component to a millimeter business. Millimeter business owners know they do not have all the answers all the time. They know that by learning just one small (millimeter) strategy or change in a particular marketing program, they can and will achieve massive results. Those millimeter changes can bring about massive profits to their businesses and get them closer to their goals.

CASE STUDY

Diane Conklin
Direct Response Marketing

I have been in direct response marketing for over 15 years and have helped many small business owners grow their businesses to six and seven figures. We always use backward planning to develop our marketing plans.

We start with our goals and the end in mind and then work backward to see exactly what we have to do to accomplish those results. We use a calendar and mind maps to work in all the details. I've never found a better way than this method to do a marketing plan. Taking this approach allows you to know on a daily basis where you are in the process. It also allows your team to be able to contribute because everyone is on the same page.

We measure results based on ROI (return on investment) and on the numbers (they don't lie and they are the only way to really know if you are on track). If your goal is $10,000 a month in revenue, and you are short of your goal one month, you will need to add the difference to the next month and reset your goals higher. It is important to stay on track and revise your goals each month if necessary to achieve your desired results. If you don't have a written plan then you don't have a plan. Stop throwing mud on the wall and just arbitrarily trying stuff. You have to have a plan that you follow, and it will make it easy for you to make decisions about what you're doing and to stay on track. ∎

CASE STUDY

Shreyans Parekh
Koyal Wholesale

I'm the Co-Founder of Koyal Wholesale, the world's largest wedding and event-supplies company (KoyalWholesale.com) that ships over 50,000 products to more than 100-plus countries worldwide. I helped to develop Koyal's marketing program in 2003 when I co-founded the company with two siblings in Southern California. Since returning back to the company in 2010 with an MBA from Wharton, I have been able to measure results using platforms such as Google Analytics and Facebook Insights.

We bootstrapped the company for several years since we lacked the capital needed for immense growth, especially in our marketing department; but since 2009, we have experienced double-digit growth in sales and staff. We started with a bold vision to revolutionize the wedding and event supplies space by implementing a fully optimized customer experience, including building a comprehensive e-commerce site, developing world-class customer service, and providing unique educational content and the world's best event products.

I spearheaded the development of our marketing plan and strategy in 2005. Since 2009, I have been able to sculpt the marketing plan accordingly over the years to cater to an increased marketing budget and spending ability that followed along with our inroads into the event planning and organization industry. We now also include in our marketing tactics programs to showcase our products and advertise throughout the U.S. and globally.

Our marketing plan has been flexible and adaptable since 2005, as it caters to seasonal trends in the wedding and event industry and leverages our website's progress. We have made numerous changes and modifications to the site annually, and we are gearing up for a site redesign and implementation that we will be rolling out shortly, which will help us to improve the overall customer experience that we offer, from ease of use and customer friendly UI to more robust order management and inventory-tracking backend.

The marketing plan has been formulated to tackle the range of platforms we use from Google Adwords and targeted ads on top wedding and event planning blogs to our social-media channels and our Southern California-based showroom to attract local wedding planners and event coordinators.

Our goals have been incrementally implemented as we have developed an intimate understanding of our customers' needs and desires for event décor and developed a greater understanding of our unique position in the wedding and event industry. There is no other company in the industry that provides a comprehensive one-stop shop for wedding and event decor needs. We have also been able to gradually increase our marketing goals and spending ability by connecting with customers through our marketing channels and gaining direct feedback on new products, content and contests to implement to gain greater exposure internationally.

Our most successful element has been our ability to create brand ambassadors for Koyal through our primary social media channels — Blog (The Daily Design by Koyal Wholesale), Facebook, Pinterest, YouTube and Instagram. We have been able to cross-promote products and our content through these channels, and analyze data and metrics associated with each of these platforms to hone our strategy moving forward. One very successful contest and promotion that we have been able to run through these channels is our bimonthly Engaged Couples Contest in which couples submit their engagement photos and their friends, family and our Facebook fans get to vote and comment on which photo they love the most. This contest has been able to generate more than 50 entries each time, and it continues to be a tremendous driver of traffic and activity to our channels and website.

We measure the results of our marketing activities and channels through Google and YouTube Analytics, and Facebook Insights. By tracking analytics daily, we have been able to really sculpt our marketing strategy to also fit seasonal trends such as bumps in traffic for summer weddings and end-of-the-year corporate events. ∎

IMPLEMENTING A "MILLIMETER APPROACH" TO YOUR MARKETING:

1. Do you have a set budget for your marketing? If not, why?
2. What has prevented you from developing a marketing plan and putting together a marketing calendar?
3. What could you do today to get a marketing plan in place? Is there a small millimeter step you can implement today that would enable your business or professional practice to acquire more customers, clients or patients?

CHAPTER 7:
MAKE YOUR PATIENTS, CLIENTS AND CUSTOMERS MEMBERS OF AA

"If you do what you've always done, you'll get what you've always gotten."
— Tony Robbins

No, I am not encouraging your customers to become members of Alcoholics Anonymous. However, I am encouraging you to make them members of an ardent admirers club. "AA" stands for "Ardent Admirers" — and it is a goal of all millimeter businesses to ensure that their customers, clients and patients are part of the club. Why should your business focus on promotions, programs and events to create Ardent Admirers? To find the answer, let's look at what advantages, opportunities and prosperity other millimeter businesses enjoy by developing their own AA membership club.

CASE STUDY

Logan Beach, Reefer's Corner Rewards Program

Reefer's Corner has a rewards program that not only gives you discounts, but also some free stuff the first time you buy anything from us. Then, we give you a 10-percent discount if you come in again, and we set you up on our program. The next time you come in we give you a choice between free five pounds of live rock, fish medication, or water conditioner. This cycle continues and the more you buy and the more you visit us the more you save and the more free stuff you get.
Now this "millimeter" approach has brought in some good clientele — and those clients have referred many people to us. They have also set up a good base and it builds on itself. ■

WHY DO YOU NEED ARDENT ADMIRERS?

A millimeter business like this one understands the importance and necessity of having Ardent Admirers. These are the customers, clients and patients who love your business and refer their friends and family. These Ardent Admirers represent the 20 percent of your business that generates 80 percent of your referrals. They are the customers, clients and patients who forgive you even when you have a "millimeter" slip in your service or communication.

Just like the above example, Ardent Admirers are developed one at a time. Millimeter businesses know that they need to take care of each and every customer like he or she is the only one they have. A millimeter business will go out of its way to make sure its communication with its customers is consistent and frequent. They understand that communication on a regular basis with real information is the key to building a strong AA membership.

How do millimeter businesses create Ardent Admirers?

They do it by making sure the millimeter things they do either with their service or product is done consistently and with passion. In the dental field, where I live, most patients are not that excited about getting crowns on their teeth. They realize they need a crown or else they could potentially lose the tooth, but the idea of a few hundred to thousands of dollars on a tooth repair is not nearly as exciting as getting a new pair of stilettos (for you ladies) or maybe a new golf club.

However, a dentist who gets the millimeter approach to developing Ardent Admirers will take the time to educate the patient on his or her decision to repair his or her tooth and get a crown. They will be passionate about what they are doing for the patient because they know that the long-term health of that tooth lies on placing a crown that fits perfectly. The patient will feel "taken care of" and that his or her new crown was a great investment in his or her dental health instead of an "unjustified" expense. A millimeter practice understands that communication and patient education are key ingredients to developing an Ardent Admirer.

Does your business communicate and educate its customers with the intent of developing Ardent Admirers?

Millimeter businesses know that Ardent Admirers are developed when the owners and employees communicate and educate their customers. Communication and education help customers feel that your business is truly interested in helping them solve their problems. With their secure feeling of trust in place, they are able to refer their closest friends and family and continue to do business with you now and in the future.

Do you have Ardent Admirers already?

Millimeter businesses will have programs in place to recognize, reward and communicate with their AA members.

What are you doing to reward, recognize and communicate with your best customers?

They offer their AA members special discounts, special opportunities and gifts for referrals, and they are given some free "stuff" in recognition of their support and confidence in their businesses. A millimeter business will do some of the following to make sure they are showing their best customers how much they truly appreciate their business and referrals.

- Provide catered lunches or dinners at your business for the AA-only customers
- Organize customer appreciation events at a local park with fun things for all the family
- Set up a private movie showing for your top customers, clients and patients
- Create special discounts only available to your AA members
- Give away gift certificates for dinner, movies or even your business
- Publish special recognition in your business newsletter either printed or emailed
- Communicate specifically to your AA members about special events
- Host special events at a winery, restaurant, water park or other fun place in your community

Of course millimeter businesses will make sure to arrange the details of these VIP events so that those that are not part of the AA membership will want to know how they too can join. Private invitations, of course, are mailed to not only those Ardent Admirers, but also the business communicates to everyone that they have an annual VIP event. The VIP event is invitation-only — and those who do not receive an invitation can learn how to get invited to the next event. Millimeter businesses understand that something as simple as a private luncheon will get everyone else wondering how they too can be part of that club.

CASE STUDY

Sarah Jo Wood
The Magic Pen Copywriting
www.evolvingadvisors.com

The biggest client appreciation program that is so often overlooked is the simple handwritten thank-you note. It means so much to the recipient. It is different because it is hardly ever done anymore. It will remain in their memories.

You can take a millimeter approach to it by adding other cards for personal events, including birthday or holiday cards. (Never put your business card in a Christmas or Hanukkah Card.) And then you can add to that with a just-thinking-of-you card, which is a special way to stay on top of their minds.

If you can, it is important to note birthdays of their children and honor those dates and their graduations as well. If you know of a promotion or other information affecting them, then a card is due, as well as a phone call. Read the papers for information about them. Find out if their favorite team is winning so when you phone you will have something to discuss. Find out their hobbies. Get to know about them other than just their businesses. Take them out for lunch or dinner, schedule permitting on their side. Or buy them a dinner coupon every few years. I try to touch clients 12-13 times a year. ■

MAKE YOUR PATIENTS, CLIENTS AND CUSTOMERS MEMBERS OF AA

CASE STUDY

Simon Tam
The Slants* Chinatown Dance Rock!

I run a number of businesses but the one that has the most engaged customer base is for The Slants. We are a touring rock band — and if there's ever a place to learn how to develop lifelong fans, it is certainly in the music industry (for example, look at diehard Kiss or Rolling Stones fans).

Many of the same lessons apply to everyday business. We offer incentives for our customers by joining our monthly email list, from discounts to free music. In addition to getting the inside scoop about the band, we also offer surprises for our followers. For example, when on tour, we pick up postcards from various cities across the country and randomly select names/addresses in our database to send them to. We simply say "hi" and "thank you" but people get really excited/appreciative and post the cards on Facebook, Instagram, etc. We like to go over the top in exceeding expectations of what a customer appreciation program is.

We continually offer specials and gifts appropriate to the season, especially during times of the year when there is less competition. For example, we like to mail out e-cards or actual red envelopes to our customers during the Lunar New Year and wish them luck. There's very little marketing "noise" in general for that holiday so it allows us to quickly cut through the clutter. Because our customers support us all year round, we believe that they should feel appreciated all year too.

I would argue that (because of our programs) we have some of the most loyal fans in the industry. People fly across the country for our events and interact with our band on a daily basis, sometimes three to five times per day on social media. Our fans then blog about us, tag us on social media, and tell others about us. We've been able to grow to an internationally recognized brand because of their enthusiasm and vigor in promoting us.

Customer appreciation programs provide a high return on investment — they are directly targeting the customer (as opposed to a blind-ad campaign). Give customers reasons to keep on coming back and they will. For our business, it has helped us launch into brand new markets fairly quickly, make us excited to interact with our customers, and allow us to build sustainable growth. ■

MAKE YOUR PATIENTS, CLIENTS AND CUSTOMERS MEMBERS OF AA

CASE STUDY

**Chuck Layman and Alicia Layman Lewis
Licensed Insurance Providers**

GrowSecure Insurance and Financial Services, office of Chuck Layman and Alicia Layman Lewis, Licensed Insurance Providers, offers Financial Security in Layman's terms and focuses on income planning in retirement. We truly value our clients and have had many different events to show our appreciation.

Our client appreciation programs have included Girls Spa Days for top female clients, an annual June Pig Roast, local hockey game tickets, Candlelight Dinner Playhouse tickets, a Holiday Party, Valentine's roses for widowed clients, and Thanksgiving pies for the holidays, and many specialized gifts for clients who have had a loss in their family, been through surgery, or just deserve a little extra treat.

Most of our programs are seasonal, but we do pay attention to specialized gifts throughout the year. The Candlelight Dinner Playhouse tickets are sent out year round depending on the show. Our Holiday Party and June Pig Roast are annual events and are held around the same time every year.

We do feel like we have created "fans" by doing this. In our business you often only see clients once a year, but by hosting these programs we get to constantly be in front of them, and we get to know them on more of a personal level. Many of our clients would not have an opportunity to go to an Eagles game or attend a pig roast if they were not our clients. People talk about our events every time we see them. They truly enjoy the community that these events provide.

Our referrals have increased since the implementation of our client appreciation events. We have positioned ourselves so we are constantly exposed to our clients and they get to know us as friends. We have opened up a few events for individuals to bring their friends and meet Chuck and Alicia in a non-threatening way. About 25 percent of our business comes from referrals. We believe our clients feel appreciated and want to give back to the business! We also take pictures at every client event and hang them in our office, mail them to clients, and even make a scrapbook that is in our conference room for our clients to view. This all contributes to our clients feeling a part of the GrowSecure family.

Overall client appreciation events make our clients feel more a part of our company community. Clients get to know each other and hang out at our various events. They get to know Chuck and Alicia out of the office and they get to do things that they may not normally do. Our client appreciation events increase referrals but they also enforce our brand. When our clients think of financial services they think of Chuck and Alicia. ∎

IMPLEMENTING A "MILLIMETER APPROACH" TO CUSTOMER, CLIENT OR PATIENT SERVICE:

1. What can you do to improve your customer care at your place of business?
2. Using a millimeter approach, write down one strategy you can implement today that would generate more potential referrals to your business or professional practice.
3. Think about your AA customers, clients or patients and what you could do to encourage, reward and recognize their efforts in helping you grow your business or professional practice.

CHAPTER 8:
EDUCATING POTENTIAL CUSTOMERS, CLIENTS AND PATIENTS IS A TOP PRIORITY OF A MILLIMETER BUSINESS

"Courage doesn't always roar. Sometimes courage is the little voice at the end of the day that says I'll try again tomorrow."
— Mary Anne Radmacher

Do you take time in your business to focus on client education? Do you write information-based newsletters and send them out to prospective business? Do you provide information, facts and figures about data related to your clients and send it, or, if you're in a profession like mine, leave it in your waiting room? Do you spend time talking to them and informing them about information related to your products and services that would bring them value and benefits?

Businesses that operate with a millimeter approach understand that educating their customers, clients or patients gives them three unique advantages:

Long-Term Clients. First, they understand that if they educate their customers, clients or patients, they will more likely keep them long term, which will entice them to purchase more products and services over their lifetimes.

More Purchases and Upgrades. Secondly, millimeter businesses know that a customer, client or patient who is educated first about a product or service is more likely to make a decision to purchase and even upgrade to a higher level of product or service based on the information they receive.

Earn Referral Business. And finally, millimeter businesses know that their customers, clients or patients will be happier and willing to refer their friends and family to your business. Why? They now have the education regarding what you offer; they are more able to share that information to their circle of influence; and they might pre-sell referrals for you.

How do I know and understand why this is important? I recently had an experience in a business that uses the millimeter approach with its customers.

I needed new cookware and specifically new sauté pans. I had been buying the same sauté pans for years, and they would last about a year and then needed replacement. I was ready to buy them again, when my husband suggested I try Sur La Table, a local store near our home that specializes in high-end products for the kitchen.

I had been educating myself a little on the benefits of some of the new type of sauté pans that were available. I had over the years been using the Teflon™-type of non-stick pans, and had learned that maybe they were not the healthiest choice for my family.

I stepped into the store and asked someone about their sauté pans and other types of cookware. The woman at the counter said she would be right back, and I assumed she would be helping me and was probably getting someone else to cover the cash register. I walked over to one section that had what I thought I was looking for, and soon a young man, around age 22 came up to me to help. His name was Nate as displayed on the nametag. I have to admit at first I thought, "Are you kidding me? A 22-year-old boy with long hair who does not even look like he eats let alone cooks is going to help me?"

Immediately, I had to take back my presumptions, as he started asking me questions about what I wanted to cook, how I cook, what types of foods I sauté, and a bunch of other questions that I was not prepared for. Okay, so maybe he was older than he looked, and he actually did cook a fair amount himself. Or maybe, the owners of Sur La Table trained him very well. Either way, I was happy he was there, and he gave me his undivided attention.

For the next 45 minutes, we went through the store, he showed me what he liked the best personally, and gave me suggestions about what would work best for me based on how and what I like to cook. He was brilliant in that he even took me to the sales section to look at La Creuset that was on sale. He told me about the great value I could receive by buying last year's "hot color."

I had not thought about buying anything other than two sauté pans, and maybe some utensils for cooking. However, Nate described to me all the great food I could make for my family and friends using the products he was recommending. His ideas were appetizing, and I, as a person who really enjoys cooking, could visualize myself making some of the dishes he was recommending.

I was hooked and ready to buy.

I decided to invest in some exceptional cookware that included some expensive sauté pans, and of course some La Creuset cookware as well. I validated the purchases based on the education provided by Nate. He shared with me the benefits that I would find in the flavor quality and health benefits of the food I would cook. He also assured me that this was an investment that I would enjoy forever. No more buying the cheaper sauté pans and replacing them every year.

He assured me that with proper care, I would have these pieces of cookware forever. (Based on the amount of money I spent, I plan to put the cookware in my will!) He was not high pressure at all, but a wealth of information. I was fascinated by this young man's knowledge of the products in the store, and his ability to get me to part with a lot more money than I had anticipated spending. As this personal example shows, education got me to upgrade beyond what I had planned to purchase — and I plan to be back for more as I replace other cookware in my kitchen. Of course that evening, I used my new pans and shared with my family the same story I have outlined here. It will most likely be a story I share with other friends who come over for dinner. Where do you think they will go to purchase new pots and pans?

This example illustrates perfectly the millimeter approach to using education as a marketing and sales tool. While Nate was not who I thought would be the one to educate me on the various types of cookware, he proved me wrong. He asked a lot of questions first to gain information about what my needs were. He did not take me to the most expensive pieces (in fact, he actually showed me the value to the Le Creuset pieces that were on sale). He mentioned that the only reason they were on sale was because of a color that was being discontinued. He knew I would want to know that and made sure to clarify it immediately. When I was leaning toward sauté pans that were actually more expensive, he educated me on the value of different pans that were more suited to my particular cooking needs.

He still ended up selling me some expensive cookware, but did it based on what he felt were the best choices for my needs. He became a trusted advisor during those 45 minutes as I could sense he had the knowledge and the passion for helping me make the best choice for my kitchen and my family.

Taking small steps to educate your customers about what products or services you have to offer is a "millimeter approach" that will prove to have a big impact on your business or professional practice.

How do they do it? There are three steps that they take:
Step 1: Ask questions and listen
Step 2: Use education-based marketing to attract business
Step 3: Hire passionate, qualified employees

STEP 1: ASK QUESTIONS AND LISTEN

First, they ask questions. In fact, they ask a lot of questions. Then they listen. Really listen without offering any advice until they have all the questions in their arsenal answered. Then they prepare to educate the customer on the best solution for them. They do this so they do not overwhelm the customer with too much information. They also know it is best to offer the most optimal solution without reference to price.

If the best solution is the cheapest, then educate them on why that is the best choice for their particular needs. If the best solution is the most expensive, then share that information with them too. You will become their trusted advisor by educating them on the specific benefits of what you offer to help them find solutions to their needs.

Once a customer feels that you have their best interests at heart, they are open to further suggestions and may start asking more questions and want to know in even greater detail about your product or service.

It is okay to offer more information, but again, as a millimeter business, you want to do this in small increments at a time. You do not want to overwhelm or "vomit" a ton of information about all 26 products or the 10 different services you offer. You will confuse them, and they may leave making a decision to not do business with you. They will feel not heard or appreciated. Unfortunately, this scenario happens way too often in businesses today. Customers, clients and patients are looking for information today about products and services. They have the ability to "Google" just about any keyword phrase to find exactly what they are looking for. Your ability to educate your prospective customer, client or patient, is another millimeter step to success.

STEP 2: USE EDUCATION-BASED MARKETING TO ATTRACT BUSINESS

Second step, millimeter businesses use education in their marketing to attract prospective customers, clients or patients to their business, store or practice. This method also keeps a steady, consistent flow of business coming in the door.

What type of educational marketing does a millimeter business do?

Many different education-based marketing tactics exist including those mentioned in the opening paragraph of this chapter. One of the best ways today to get prospective customers interested in what you have to offer is through the use of video. Simple, short videos found on either your website, You Tube, Facebook page, blogs or other Internet-related media, will set you apart from the rest of your competition.

The millimeter approach to successful implementation of an educational marketing strategy is to have videos created that answer the questions most of your customer base requests. For example, for our practice website, www.luvmysmile.com, I did a short three-minute video that answered the questions regarding the difference between metal braces and Invisalign™.

We used the video features on my iPhone, and it took about one hour of preparation and 10 minutes of videotaping. The prep work was the most frequently asked questions that I hear from patients all day long. I wanted to make sure I covered the majority of those questions. It was a simple, cost-effective video, which did not require thousands of dollars to produce. As a result, it has attracted many patients who were searching for that information. These patients wanted Invisalign, but were not sure about its benefits versus traditional metal braces.

The millimeter approach would be to get these educational videos up on your website as soon as possible. The most important part of the videos is the information you share. Make sure to write down all the questions you hear every day coming from your customers, clients or patients. Get started today, with a short video that answers those most commonly asked questions.

Along with videos, make sure you have written materials that fully educate your potential customers, clients and patients about your products or services. Make sure you can customize that information to suit their needs. For example, if you are a dentist and a patient comes to your office for a consultation, and after you do the initial evaluation, she shares that her biggest concern is all her missing teeth. You ask more questions about what bothers her most. Is it the cosmetic aspect? Maybe she is having trouble eating and other teeth are becoming increasingly worn down. Dig deeper to find out her biggest concern. Ask questions and listen.

Then you can start to take the millimeter approach by offering her your professional opinion about the best solutions that would fit her lifestyle and needs. You might suggest dental implants. Have an educational written piece to give her. Have before and after photos of successful implant cases. Include testimonials from your patients who have had successful implants. If she is concerned about cost, make sure you have information available about financing so that she can make monthly payments.

No matter your product or service, you need to make sure there is plenty of information available for you and your employees to share with prospective customers. Just like the videos that you create, the written material does not have to be fancy or printed. Just write down the most commonly asked questions about your product or service and have great testimonials added to the content. That is simply all you need to do.

You can repurpose the information as well in ads that you may place in select media. You may also use it in your other communication methods such as newsletters and email that go out to your customer base on a regular basis.

STEP 3: HIRE PASSIONATE, QUALIFIED EMPLOYEES

The third and final step is often the most challenging for businesses. Businesses that take a millimeter approach have employees who are knowledgeable and passionate about the products or services they represent. They know that this does not come from being "lucky" when hiring or happen without effort.

Millimeter businesses know that it takes training, training again, and even more training to develop their employees' level of knowledge and expertise. They realize it is not a one-time event that occurs only with new hires, but it is an ongoing process that requires consistent training, workshops and continuing education to keep their team of employees working toward the best they can be.

As a millimeter business, you also have hired employees who are passionate about what they do. They take ownership of the product or service your business offers. Just like my experience with Nate, he was not only knowledgeable, but also very passionate about great cookware and the benefits (great food) that come with it. His excitement about the different products and his ability to share with me how he uses them to prepare great meals, helped me visualize myself doing the same thing.

Are your employees knowledgeable and passionate about your products or service? Are they able to help your potential customer visualize himself or herself using or experiencing your product or service?

I would say that YOU also need to be knowledgeable and passionate about your products or service. I know this seems like a "duh!" moment, but often I find that a business lacks passion because the leader (the owner) has none. If this represents you, you need to get the PASSION back before you can get your employees passionate. It starts from the top, and the employees will go along with the training and workshops, but fail to hold onto their passion consistently without the leader demonstrating it on a daily basis.

In conclusion, these three steps, asking questions, providing education through effective marketing, and making sure you and your team of employees has the knowledge and passion to help your business grow, are all key components and top priorities for millimeter businesses.

IMPLEMENTING A "MILLIMETER APPROACH" TO EDUCATING YOUR CUSTOMERS, CLIENTS AND PATIENTS:

1. Do you have educational materials for your potential clients, customers or patients that will answer their questions and concerns?

2. Are you passionate about your product or service? Are your employees passionate about what you offer?
3. What can you do immediately to start better educating your potential customers, clients and patients about your products or services?

CHAPTER 9:
MILLIMETER BUSINESSES FOCUS ON EXCEPTIONAL EXPERIENCES

*"Some people dream of great accomplishments
while others stay awake and do them."*
— Anonymous

In the last chapter, we learned that a millimeter approach to business requires a focus on educating your potential customer, client or patient. In this chapter, the focus will be on providing exceptional experiences for your customers, clients or patients. In reality, both education and exceptional experiences go hand-in-hand.

A customer may come into your restaurant and ask the waiter about the difference between two chardonnays. The waiter may educate the customer about the wines, one being fruity and the other more buttery. However, by adding the experience of tasting both, the customer now has a better idea which one they like and will most likely place an order.

In the last chapter, Nate from Sur La Table offered to have me try out the sauté pans he recommended. The store had a burner set up and the pans ready for action. I could literally try them out in the store to see how I liked the way they worked. I actually declined the offer only because he had done such a great job of educating me about the pans — and I trusted him completely. The store, however, took a millimeter approach by having the opportunity to experience the pans right there in the store. This is what sets a millimeter business apart from the rest.

What type of experience does a millimeter business provide?

Let me start by sharing what we have done in our orthodontic practice to give our patients experiences to remember. Most orthodontic and dental offices are considered to be places where you will have pain. Maybe the pain is from the tightening of the braces or a new stronger wire being placed onto the braces themselves. The pain could come from the teeth cleaning or maybe a new cavity needs to be filled. There is also fear about what is going to happen to them once they step into the office.

As an orthodontist, I know my patients are thinking, "Is the doctor going to make my teeth hurt?" They may be worried that they are going to get "molds" of their teeth and have nasty, goopy stuff that makes them gag when placed in their mouths. We want to make those thoughts disappear by providing an experience for the patients that is fun and enjoyable when they come in for their orthodontic appointments.

What do we do to provide a fun experience?

We have contests that they can enter to win different prizes. For example, we posted on our bulletin board pictures of all our pets, both doctors' pets and staff members' pets. We had pictures of the staff and a sheet they could fill out each time they came in that would allow them to guess which pet went with the staff member. They were permitted to enter the contest each visit and whoever guessed the most correct, won an iPod Touch. It was a lot of fun for everyone to try and figure out who had which pet. It was fun for my staff to see how the parents and patients associated different pets with different members of my team.

Another time we did the same thing with shoes. That was even harder for the patients and parents. Except for my husband, the entire staff is women, so it was a real challenge to match with team members. Again, they could enter the contest each time they had an appointment, and we would run the contest for three months at a time.

We host fun events in our office.

In the summer, we have ice cream sundae day. Patients can stop by with no appointment needed and have a free ice cream sundae. My teenage children help manage the event, and they are always amazed how many people show up for free ice cream. We encourage our patients to bring friends who are not even patients to the office for the free sundaes. It is a great way to bring potential patients into our practice. They see it is a fun place and that we are not just about braces.

Other fun events we host include Root Beer Float Day, Mad Science Day, Decorate Cupcake Day and Pictures with Santa Day. Our patients are informed of all these events via email and our practice newsletter.

We also participate in community-sponsored events.

We are members of our local chambers of commerce and participate in many of their community events. These events are a great way to interact with your community and provide excellent opportunities to let the community know more about who you are and what you offer.

Make sure to have a drawing or some other exciting opportunity at your booth for the people attending these events. We have rented photo booths and have people register their address and email in order to go into the booth and get their photos taken. This results in a new database for us to use for future mailings and other communication.

We provide a wheel they can spin for prizes or they also can enter their names for a drawing to win prizes like free teeth whitening or free retainers. We email our patients in advance and let them know we will be at these different community events and stop by and visit us.

We are big on giving gifts. Patients (children) who come in for an initial consultation receive a gift bag filled with goodies including our practice newsletter, a coupon for a free consultation, logo pens and pencils and other fun stuff. The parents or adult patients, receive a book, written by yours truly, *Healthy and Beautiful At Any Age, Your Smile and Modern Orthodontics*. This is given to them right at the start of their new patient exam and consultation. The book educates them on everything they need to know about orthodontics. They leave the office loaded with great information and gifts.

When a patient begins treatment in our office, we send flowers to the dental office that referred them to us. The flowers are delivered with a beautiful thank-you card. The referring dental office loves the flowers at the front desk, and of course, the patients who come to that office get to enjoy them as well.

The patients who get started with braces or Invisalign also receive a gift from us. Cookies are delivered to their homes with a thank-you card for choosing our practice for their orthodontic needs.

We also give gifts at the end of treatment to thank them for helping us achieve a healthy and beautiful new smile and letting them know we appreciate their referrals of family and friends.

We host patient-appreciation parties. Once a year, we will host patient-appreciation events to honor and thank our patients for their support, confidence and referrals to our practice.

We have rented out movie theaters, roller-skating rinks and community parks to provide an exceptional and unexpected experience for our patients and their families.

The buzz created from these events helps to keep our phones ringing and our schedule full of new patients in our practice.

We have fun as a team of professionals. To ease our patients' fears and worries, we make sure to always smile and have a friendly and warm attitude. This attitude comes from our staff and the doctors who have been trained on bringing joy and fun into the clinical area where the patients have the most fear. In a typical orthodontic practice, the dental chairs are in an open bay so that everyone can see and hear what is happening with the next patient. This permits us to have fun, entertaining conversations that are good for everyone to hear. By having an atmosphere where everyone is sharing stories and communication, the patients get involved and enjoy the atmosphere of camaraderie.

By training and encouraging our team members to have fun, be friendly and be open, the patients feel more at ease and less fearful. They are more relaxed and end up enjoying their visit to our offices. Once what was fearful and worrisome becomes an attitude of "I can't wait to go back!"

How can you implement these ideas?
How can your business provide exceptional experiences to your customers?

Here are examples of a few businesses that have provided these experiences to their customers using a millimeter approach.

CASE STUDY

Dev Piprottar
General Manager
Best Western Luxbury Inn

At Best Western Luxbury Inn, a top-rated hotel in Fort Wayne, IN, we train our employees to provide the best possible guest experience with two things in mind: First, our goal is to make the guest a loyal, permanent customer; and second, we have heart in serving the customer.

The guest must be greeted with a cheerful voice when the guest is within 15 feet from the front desk. We have a slogan: "When a guest is waiting, the world stops." Guests must be attended immediately. Guests must be acknowledged upon arrival even if you are busy with another guest. Make sure to take care of the current guest properly without rushing, but also efficiently without making the guest feel rushed or making the waiting guest feel that you are taking your time and not caring about other guests in line. Any request must be followed up ASAP and the guest must be updated about the status, if it cannot be fixed or resolved immediately.

We know our programs work. We became the number one hotel on tripadvisor.com out of 48 hotels within 10 months. Since then, we have always been number one or two, we even have four brand new hotels in Fort Wayne, IN.

We monitor our programs and make small, but necessary changes when appropriate. But there is no question our programs work. It's your heart. When you put your heart into something people will notice. We will always continue to refine our program. If any guest mentions any of our associates' names on tripadvisor.com, the associate is entitled to $20 cash or a gift certificate. ∎

CASE STUDY

Jessica Carstens
Marketing Associate
Cartelligent

At Cartelligent, we help our clients have the best car-buying experience of their lives. Our Client Experience Managers help them decide which make and model will best meet their needs, then our team of buyers source the car and negotiates with multiple dealers to get them a great price. Finally the client picks up the car at one of our convenient locations and a Client Care Specialist walks them through paperwork, shows them the features of their new car, and even syncs the car with their Bluetooth device.

We do extensive client surveying to ensure that the Cartelligent experience is a great one and solicit feedback on how we can improve our process. We slowly adjust our programs to ensure their success. We originally had the Client Experience Manager doing the sourcing and the walk through as well as the consultations and follow up. As we grew, we separated the jobs out in order to allow each person to truly be an expert in his or her specialty.

We're always open to making our clients' experiences with Cartelligent better and are constantly striving to improve our training. ■

IMPLEMENTING A "MILLIMETER APPROACH" TO EXCEPTIONAL EXPERIENCES:

1. What can you do to enhance your customer, client or patient experience?
2. What programs or training will be necessary to achieve a significant change in the way your employees communicate with your customers?
3. Is there a small step you can take today to improve your customer, client or patient experience that will provide a big impact on your business or professional practice?

PART 2
IT'S ALL ABOUT MILLIMETERS AND LIFE

CHAPTER 10:
A MILLIMETER APPROACH TO LEADERSHIP

"Think small, work hard, get good."
— George Gilder

A search on the Internet reveals there are over 50-trillion books written on leadership. It is obviously a very hot topic! There are so many great authors who I admire tremendously. I will not try to even compete with some of the greatest authors in this category, but instead share my personal journey on the quest to become a better and more effective leader by using a millimeter approach.

I never thought about being a leader or that I was a leader until about a decade ago. There was never any discussion in dental school regarding leadership or required reading on leadership. As health-care professionals, we are certainly in leadership positions in our communities. However, just because there is a DDS (or a DMD in my case) behind my name, did not grant me honorary leadership skills.

The bottom line is as a business or practice owner, we are leaders whether we know it or not.

So what is leadership and what makes a person a great leader?

For purposes of my discussion here, I found this definition from the U.S. Air Force to most closely represent the leadership that I will be discussing in this chapter. "Leadership is the art of influencing and directing people in such a way that will win their obedience, confidence, respect and loyal cooperation in achieving common objectives."

The qualities of a great leader are many. Here are just a few that I feel personally are "must-have" qualities of a great leaders.

Integrity represents the integration of inner values with actions. A person of integrity will follow their inner values at all times, even if it is the difficult choice.

Dedication in a leader means setting an example for others to follow. A leader will do whatever it takes to accomplish the task and those around him or her will be inspired by that dedication.

Humility is the ability of a leader to give credit to those who have helped him or her succeed. They know that they cannot do it alone. They elevate everyone around them to new levels of performance and productivity.

Trustworthiness in a leader means you will do what you said you would do. In other words, you keep your promises to your family, employees, friends, customers, clients and patients.

Listening first before speaking is another essential quality of a leader. Great leaders are open to new ideas and ways of solving problems. In fact, they encourage it among their employees. They know that developing the ability to listen closely is the most important way to make the people around them feel heard and recognized.

Creative thinking is another quality great leaders exhibit. They think out of the box and are willing to try new strategies to get the job done.

Immunity to criticism is another leadership trait. A great leader will not succumb to popular opinion just to avoid criticism. If they know that they will receive criticism for something they have implemented, they are willing to face it head on and not be swayed by it.

Decisiveness versus procrastination is another quality of a great leader. Making decisions quickly and without "paralysis by analysis" is important for great leaders.

Productivity and Focus are also important traits of great leaders. When those around you see your focus and ability to get things done, they will follow in your footsteps.

Passion for your business, practice, your career, your friends and family that is obvious and contagious is another quality of a great leader.

Finally, **a sense of humor** and the ability to not take themselves too seriously is vital to relieve tension and diffuse hostility. Effective leaders will use humor to energize their employees, and this fosters greater teamwork.

Of course there are at least a dozen more qualities of a great leader. Entire books have been written about just one of the above that I have highlighted. I encourage you to take some time to build your leadership library. There is no shortage of great books! However, for purposes of this chapter, I want to share my personal journey in becoming a better leader and hope to inspire you to develop your leadership skills, or if you have started already, to keep on the journey.

THE LEADERSHIP JOURNEY

Growing as a leader is a journey, not a destination. My growth started much later in my career than I like to admit. Unfortunately, it is true. I never wanted to be a leader. I always thought of myself as a good listener and someone who could follow directions quite well. A leader? No way!

When I opened my first practice in the late 1980's, if you remember, it was a tremendous struggle to succeed. Besides not having any knowledge or experience in business, marketing or managing employees, I was lacking in real leadership skills. I never understood that employees need a strong leader to succeed. I never understood that for a business or professional practice to succeed in an extraordinary way, a strong leader was needed at the forefront.

So when did I figure this out?

I am embarrassed to admit it, but it wasn't until 2005 that I finally figured out that I needed to change something … and that something was ME!

We had a successful practice, but we were constantly hiring, training, and then terminating employees. I would hire office managers who were supposed to make my job easier and instead, they made my life more stressful. How did this happen? I abdicated all my leadership to them. Have you done this? Are you still doing this? By the end of this chapter, you will find out there is a different path to follow.

After I had terminated yet another office manager who I thought was a strong leader and very capable, I realized the problem was not all those previous office managers. The problem was me. I was hiring the wrong people and hoping they would take over the job that I really did not want. And what was that job? Being the LEADER of my practice.

I have to admit, once I figured out the problem was with me, I was a bit depressed. I had hoped I could "turf" all the responsibility of running my practice to someone else. I was paying them a fantastic salary and gave them loads of freedom to make decisions, handle employee problems, and deal with everything other than treating patients. I figured if I had a key person in charge I could just do my orthodontics and the rest would fall into place. I found out this was not true.

What did I do?

I took a millimeter approach to becoming a leader. Not just any leader, but a leader who would be able to influence and direct people and win their obedience, confidence and loyalty to achieve common objectives. Once I had this skill set, I knew I would have an extraordinary practice and life. Let me share with you how I did this.

I started reading books on leadership. There are 50 trillion of them so I figured I would start simply by reading. I set a goal to get through a leadership book a month. You can set your own goals, but get started. With a millimeter approach it does not matter whether you read one book a week, month, quarter or even year. You will learn skills that you can implement with a small effort, but produce big results. That is the millimeter way.

My journey included books from Zig Ziglar, John Maxwell, Stephen Covey, John Wooden, Brian Tracy, Tony Robbins, Chet Holmes, Dan Kennedy, Rudy Guiliani, Billy Graham, Napoleon Hill and Dale Carnegie to name a few.

I also rented, borrowed from friends or just purchased audio series on leadership that I could listen to in my car. To this day, it is rare for me to have the radio on. My children will often say, "Mom, can't we just listen to music today?" Even though they hate it, I know I am building leaders in them a millimeter at a time, too, as they ride in the car to and from school or other errands. I suggest trying it for yourself and see how you and your children all together become better leaders.

These authors and many more were my constant companions, either in book or audio form, in my journey to become a leader. One small step at a time, I started to feel and see a change.

What were the changes?

First, I felt mentally stronger and more secure about who I was. When you start to dive into the leadership world and read about others who have succeeded despite poor beginnings, you gain confidence in yourself. You realize that if they can do it, so can you. That is why throughout this book I have placed stories about other people and their businesses. When you read about someone else's journey, it gives you a vision about what is possible for you. When I would read, I visualized myself in similar situations and would find my own solutions to problems that were similar.

Second, I began to learn new skills. The authors would share strategies, tactics and techniques that they were using to accomplish their leadership goals. I would pick out those strategies and tactics that I felt would help me grow my leadership muscles. I would often lapse back into my old ways of doing things, which included avoidance, procrastination, denial and indecision. These behaviors were my faithful and comfortable companions. I learned that setbacks were inevitable and part of the journey. I would, of course, beat myself up — I had failed to do the right thing.

MILLIMETER APPROACH TO SUCCESS

If you use a millimeter approach, you realize that you have not failed. You just took a small step back to your old comfort zone. You will be re-focused the next time on using the right leadership approach when faced with the opportunity to do so. Speaking of comfort zone, a third big area of change was my ability to step out of my comfort zone.

How much do we hate to do that? No one really likes to do it, but that is where the true growth occurs. Because I have such a fear of stepping out of the safety of my circle, I would just attempt one small out-of-the-box strategy at a time. By doing it in small steps, it did not seem like such a huge undertaking. That is where the millimeter approach was working in my leadership growth, one millimeter at a time.

How many times have we avoided doing something that we knew we had to do but did not have the courage to move forward? For me, it was employees who I knew needed to be terminated as they are were not productive and did not represent our practice's mission and values. Sometimes, these employees were actually harming my practice and causing patients to go elsewhere. Sometimes they were causing friction among other employees who ended up resigning due to the stress in the office.

Sound familiar to your business or professional practice?

In my coaching with private clients, this is one of the toughest areas of growth and development, being able to fire unproductive employees who often are sabotaging their practices. It is never a fun task to terminate an employee, but it is one of those leadership skills that must be developed and implemented if you are going to be successful in your business or practice. There is too much competition today for the consumer's wallets to have anyone working for you that is not performing their jobs at peak performance.

This leads me to the fourth change that occurred for me in my leadership development, and that was my ability to communicate and delegate effectively to my employees. Again this was a huge area of growth for me — this skill required me to let go of overseeing every single aspect of my practice. As business owners and professionals, we often like to micro-manage our employees. By overseeing every little aspect of an employee's job, you might think that this is a good approach, but a millimeter business understands that it does not work in the long run.

As a business or practice leader, you need to develop the leader in your employees. This can be done with a millimeter approach. I realized that I could get more accomplished by delegating to key employees certain tasks — and this would allow me to be more productive and focus on only those things that would generate income. When I put my employees in charge of certain aspects of our practice whether it was scheduling, collecting insurance money, or performing a specific marketing tactic, they began to take ownership of the task — and they, too, grew in their leadership skills. Now they were the go-to person for this particular area of the practice. I expected them to handle problems, create more efficient ways of doing a certain task, produce monthly reports on their activities, and report on the associated results.

It created an individual who not only had accountability, but also was given the ability to suggest alternative, more effective ways to handle the particular task or solve a particular problem. It empowered my employees to do more and be more. In turn, they too developed new leadership muscles and thrived. This is a key component of being a strong leader.

A final change that came about due to my new focus on leadership had to do with taking responsibility for what happened at the office and in my personal and family life as well. I was not aware that my actions or lack of decisiveness, would affect those around me. What I discovered, however, was how much my ability to lead and set an example would raise everyone around me to greater levels of productivity and performance (including my own children).

There is a sense of security that comes when someone is in charge, whether as the owner of a business, professional practice or even the leader of a household who exhibits the qualities of a great leader. The truth is, being a leader and developing your leadership skills takes time, commitment and a millimeter approach. With over 50-trillion books written on the subject, it is an important topic and one that millions of people want to learn more about. How come that with all those books, we have a shortage of true leadership in business and in the world today?

Think about how much the lack of leadership has caused our current problems today in the United States. As I am writing this book, we are still in a severe economic decline that has lasted over four years and no elected officials want to take responsibility for it. Think about major companies and their lack of leadership: employees losing jobs; CEOs going to jail and more and more evidence of corruption and dishonesty. Where are the leaders in all of this?

Finally, as a business owner, does your business need new leadership to help it get out of the slump it is in? Would becoming a better leader help your employees be more excited about working for you? Would becoming a better leader bring new energy, excitement, productivity and passion to your business? Do you think that would help your ultimate bottom line?

Becoming the leader you were meant to be does not happen overnight. It happens a millimeter at a time. However, those millimeter steps to becoming a better leader will bring huge changes in your business and personal life.

IMPLEMENTING A "MILLIMETER APPROACH" TO YOUR LEADERSHIP SKILLS:

1. What qualities listed above do you feel you need to work on to become the leader you want to be?
2. Do you see areas in your business or professional practice where better leadership could make a huge difference in your employees' productivity and your overall profitability?

3. What small millimeter changes can you make today in your leadership that would have a big impact in your business or professional practice?

CHAPTER 11:

MILLIMETERS AND TIME MANAGEMENT EQUALS POWERFUL PERSONAL PRODUCTIVITY

"All great changes are preceded by chaos."
— Deepak Chopra

This chapter's subject matter happens to be one of my personal favorite topics. Why?

Because, thinking about getting it all done a millimeter at a time has been the way I have operated for the past five years.

Okay, if you noticed, I said past the five years…what happened before that? Honestly, I was not very productive and wasted literally thousands of hours of my life on things that I should have delegated, deleted or deferred to another time and place. I was unable to give up many of my "tasks" because I felt I was the only one who could get them done and done right. Can you relate?

In this chapter I am going to share with you my journey to a millimeter approach to time management. I believe you will find a few ideas that will help you manage your time more effectively and therefore increase your personal productivity.

Let's start with how I managed my time before using a millimeter approach.

I would start my day checking email and say to myself, "Okay, I am going to just do a quick check and 'knock' out a few responses." Sometimes 30-45 minutes would pass before I realized that I had wasted valuable early morning time on relatively unimportant emails.

I would look up at the clock and realize that I now had no time to do my reading, workout or write that article. In fact, I was late waking up my children for school, and now they were behind schedule. Panic mode set in because they needed breakfast, I had not made their lunches, and they were running around asking me why the printer would not work. They had homework to print out and they too waited until the last minute to get it done — and now they were upset that they might be late for school. I would quickly hop in the shower, throw on clothes and make-up, pull my hair back into a ponytail, and re-enter the frantic morning pace. Finally the printer worked, the homework was completed, and now it was a race to school, hoping that there would be no traffic, no highway patrol and no red lights.

Kids safely deposited at school, off to the office, and a quick drive to Starbucks for a coffee and pastry for breakfast. Now I was late for our morning staff meeting — and I remember I needed to remind them of a few schedule changes, but by the time I got in, they had already done it without me and started with patients. I walked back into my private office for a quick breather and down my coffee and pastry. I tried to talk with my mouth full, as one of my employees comes to me and fills me in on the latest issue regarding an unhappy parent. It was a scheduling issue and they wanted a certain day and time and unfortunately my team could not accommodate them. The discussion went on for 15 minutes followed by another team member "dumping" different problems on my lap.

Of course, I finally made it out of the private office and into the clinical area, but the dumping would continue all the way through the morning. By the end of the day, I was drained by the non-stop "problems" brought directly to me. Lunchtime came and before I left, I did a quick check of my emails and any voicemails that came through in the morning. Again, rather than leaving the office and getting a real break, I now had less than 30 minutes to grab a sandwich before patients started up in the afternoon.

More employees dumping as the afternoon continued and every time I would go back into my private office for a breather or to return a phone call, there was an unexpected and unscheduled interruption. It was hard to stay focused with so many fires burning for me to put out.

It was the end of the day, with a quick stop at Starbucks again for another coffee. I remembered there was not much in the refrigerator for dinner so I quickly stopped at the grocery store before going home to cook. There was dinner to make, one child not home yet and needed to be picked up from water polo practice (delegated to my husband), and homework to get done.

I had some charting to do that I did not have time to do while seeing patients and needed to get it done after dinner. Dinner was served, dishes were done, and homework started. I decided to check my email and Facebook just briefly and then get started on my patient charting. Again, what I expected to take 15 minutes ended up being 40 minutes on the Internet. The charting never got done, as I was now too tired to keep my eyes open and needed to get the kids to bed and begin another day.

Sound familiar? If you are a working parent you may relate to my story about getting kids ready for school and doing homework at night. For others reading this, you may relate more to the stories about employees dumping problems and interrupting you all day long. And finally, there are those of you addicted to emailing, texting, reviewing Facebook, and going over other media that pulls you away from the important tasks that need to get done.

WHAT IS YOUR TIME WORTH?

You see, I had a real problem and it had to do with a lack of respect for my time. I felt my time was not worth much by my actions and the way I spent my time. Let's look at this more closely.

Albert Einstein is quoted as saying, "Insanity is doing the same things over and over again and expecting different results."

Yes, I was practicing insanity. I kept thinking that things would change, my schedule would improve, and that my frantic pace would slow down. But I failed to answer the key question, "How valuable is my time?" Once I had a clear answer as to what my time was worth, I began to respect it and treat it as a very valuable commodity, like precious gold.

Now I want you to ask yourself: What is your time worth?

You can get an idea of how much your time is worth per hour by figuring out how much you earn per year or would like to earn. For example, if you currently earn $100,000 a year, take that number and divide by 12 months. You get a monthly income of $8333. Take that number and divide by 20 days in a month that you work. You will get $417 per day. Then take that number and divide by seven hours per day of productive work and you get $60 per hour. This number is just an approximate value of what your time is worth — and a very simple formula that I have used with my coaching clients. Of course, you can change the parameters to fit your ideal workweek as well, but the idea is to figure out how much your time is worth.

There is the value you place on your time regardless of the monetary factor. As I have celebrated birthdays each year, I realize how quickly they come around and also how rapidly time is speeding by. Each day now is more valuable to me as I have gotten older. Why wait to value your time? Start right now to put a value on your time and how you use it as a precious commodity not to be wasted.

A MILLIMETER APPROACH TO TIME MANAGEMENT

Once you start to place a real value on your time, you begin to understand how important it is to use it wisely. When thinking about millimeters and how small steps can produce big results, I realized that a millimeter approach to time management would improve my personal productivity and reduce my stress.

Here is the millimeter approach to time management that I have implemented to increase my personal productivity.

Step 1: Figure out what your time is worth to you.

This could be a real number, a number you would like it to be, or no number at all just priceless.

Write it down somewhere you can see it daily.

Step 2: Learn to block your time.

For example, if I have patients to see, I have my staff schedule them in a tight block of time, so that when I am in the office, I am seeing patients and that is the main focus of my time. I want to be able to focus 100 percent of my time on my patients. I block out time for administrative duties as well. During this time, I am charting, making follow-up calls, checking emails, writing articles for my newsletters, and planning my marketing and treatment plan for my orthodontic cases.

I have time blocked out to meet with other dentists, meet with my staff, and meet with vendors and other salespeople.

I also block time for other projects. For example, writing this book. I would block time weekly so that I could complete this book on time. I block time out for working out, getting my hair cut, spending time with my spouse and children and other fun activities.

Step 3: Learn to control your interruptions.

Getting up in the morning and checking my email does not happen anymore for me. I have specific times in the day that my email and voicemail are checked. If I was waiting for a response and I need it by 10:00 a.m., I may check to see if that person replied. However, I do not go on to my email just because it is there. The same goes for Facebook and other social media. I have certain days of the week that I will check those sites or have it delegated to key employees

In any case, set a timer and stay focused. You will be amazed when you set a specific time (say 15 minutes) to check and reply to email how quickly that alarm sounds. When you start doing this, you will get much more efficient at checking email and Facebook. You realize your time is valuable and you need to get the information and move on quickly.

Also, it is important to control interruptions from employees during the day. I no longer allow them to just wander into my office and dump. If there is a situation that needs my immediate attention, they know there is a specific time right after lunch they can come to me and speak with me about it. Otherwise, all dumping now occurs at our monthly three-hour staff meeting and workshop.

By controlling who and what enters your conscious space, you will control your time more effectively. You will be able to group similar activities together and get them done more quickly. Likewise, your employees will learn to handle some of the issues that come up on their own, especially if you make yourself less available to them.

They too will see your time management skills at work and learn to operate more like you. That will translate into more efficient and productive employees.

Step 4: Delegate, delegate, delegate

This one was the hardest for me! You need to let go of stuff that someone else can do and let them just do it.

Instead of "scrubbing toilets" on a Saturday, hire a cleaning crew to come in and clean once a week. Remember what your time worth is. Instead of spending a day cleaning your house, you could be going to the gym, spending time with your spouse or significant other, watching your kids play soccer or just resting.

What else can you delegate? Grocery shopping, cooking, checking emails, opening mail, getting your car washed, picking up kids from school, driving kids around to activities, shopping for gifts, decorating for the holidays, wrapping gifts, etc. — and you get the picture. Think of all the things you do that could be delegated and free up your time to do more valuable activities. Activities that will make you more money or give you more free time to do those things you want to do.

Colleagues ask me all the time how I manage to get so much done. I tell them besides my dental degree I also have an MD degree. No not a medical doctor, but a "Master of Delegation" degree. I earned it the hard way. By refusing to hire help or delegate tasks to key employees, my spouse and even my children, I was the champion of doing it all myself. I wore that title like a badge of honor. It eventually became more like the badge of burnout.

If you have employees, start delegating more to them. You will be amazed how they thrive with the new levels of responsibility. If you are a "solo-preneur," I highly recommend a personal assistant. You will find plenty of college-age men and women who are looking for a job. I have found personally that they are a great source for personal assistants because of their flexible schedules and computer skills. Your local community college will usually have a job board or some other media available to advertise a position.

Step 5: Delete those activities that are non-productive and time wasters.

Take a good look at a typical day and see where you have wasted precious time doing something that was not that important at all. Was it running to the post office to get stamps instead of ordering them directly online and having them shipped to your office? Did you make two trips to the grocery store because you forgot a key ingredient for the dinner you had planned?

You can avoid some of these unnecessary activities by having your day planned in advance. You should have a calendar that blocks out time for all your activities that you decide you are going to get done. Stick to your agenda and you will find that it gets easier and easier to follow your blocked-out plan.

Activities that you thought were important can be deleted, because you have found a better, more efficient way they can get accomplished.

Step 6: Take your "to-do" list three items at a time.

Again, another hard one for me, but this is where the millimeter approach really kicks in.

We all have these long lists of things to do. They can be both business related and personal. Needless to say, we all tend to list them all and look at the paper and immediately get overwhelmed.

Try picking three things at a time that you will get done. Once those three are done, you get to do three more. I suggest only three a day. If you get all three done by 10:00 a.m., then go ahead and do three more. Trust me on this one, when you just focus on three projects, you will stop feeling overwhelmed. I suggest having a master list and from that list, write down the three goals you have for your day. Once those are accomplished, go back to your master list for three more.

This will empower you to feel like you are getting your projects handled and your goals accomplished. A long list that seems to never get shorter is a recipe for overwhelm and discouragement.

Step 7: Plan ahead

If you are looking at your week ahead on a Sunday afternoon, you should take five to 10 minutes to plan not only your schedule, but also your kid's schedule, and maybe key employees' time as well.

If you are a mom reading this, try to plan your meals for the week. Make a big batch of lasagna or meatballs on Sunday that can be dinner for a few nights. (It is the Italian in me speaking here about food.) Plan on shopping for all you will need for lunches and breakfast too during the week. Avoiding unnecessary trips to the grocery store is key to successful use of your precious time. Of course, you can delegate the shopping and even the cooking to free up your time for more productive activities. Get your family involved in preparing or planning a dinner.

Our teenage daughter now cooks one night a week for the family and actually enjoys it.

If you want to get to the gym or workout at home, put it in your calendar the actual time and day. Make it part of your schedule and stick to it. Respect your time and your calendar. Look at time slots that you have available and see if you can be more efficient with your time. Are there activities that you can delegate, delete or defer to another week, month or year?

Respect every minute of your time and realize that even a few minutes here or there wasted can add up to hours, days or even months of time that could have been spent doing things that are more productive or more fun for you. By planning ahead, you will save valuable time because you are prepared for the week in front of you.

Step 8: Use unexpected free time wisely.

Have you ever had 10 minutes while waiting for someone either at work or at home?

Do you realize you can get some serious work accomplished in those 10 minutes? Again, I use the "rule of three:" get three things done quickly and move on to three more. If you are home, you can load the dishwasher, unload the dishwasher, or make lunches for the next day. At the office, you can return a phone call, go through mail or plan your goals for the next day.

The rule of three works very well in these situations especially if you just take action. Do not think and plan too much, just do.

This works well for your children too. If you have 10 minutes, before dinner, set an alarm and have them do three things in that timeframe. If they get it done before the alarm goes off, you can reward them with extra dessert or cash or whatever you choose. It is a fun activity with children and gets them excited to help you around the house or even at your office.

Step 9: Learn to say no.

Another big, tough one for me!

I would say yes to everything and everybody all the time. As you become more efficient with your time and people see you get things done, you will have more and more opportunities presented to you. All the opportunities will look and feel incredible. At first you will say yes, yes, yes to all of them. Please step back and evaluate them first.

Some opportunities will be easy to say yes to because they will not require too much of your time or minimal investment of money. The ones I am talking about are the ones that will require a big time investment and possibly a large monetary one as well. You need to go back and look at what your time is worth and your goals for your personal, professional or business life and see if it is a good fit.

Step 10: Write down all my tips!

If you have not written down or highlighted these nine steps, I suggest that you do so immediately. My millimeter approach is not too complicated, but does require you to think about your time, how to respect it more, and how to make those changes in your daily routine.

Again, those small changes will have a huge impact in your life as you manage your time more effectively.

IMPLEMENTING A "MILLIMETER APPROACH" TO PERSONAL PRODUCTIVITY:

1. Do you know what your time is worth? If not, go ahead and do the math that I outlined in this chapter and write down the dollar amount somewhere you can see it on a regular basis.
2. What is your biggest challenge when it comes to managing your time effectively?
3. What small millimeter changes can you make today that would have a big impact in your personal productivity?

CHAPTER 12:
A MILLIMETER APPROACH TO RELATIONSHIPS

*"They always say time changes things,
but you actually have to change them yourself."*
— Andy Warhol

Would you like to build stronger, longer lasting, more committed relationships with your customers, clients and patients? What would it look like if you were able to have more engaged and motivated employees? How would it feel to have more loving relationships with your family, spouse, children and friends? Of course, all of the above is possible with a millimeter approach to relationships.

Let's get started with what I call the "Five Key Steps to Relationship Building with a Millimeter Approach."

STEP ONE: SMILE OFTEN. LAUGH OUT LOUD.

Have you ever had someone just smile at you for no reason? What did you do? You most likely smiled back, and the smile came without really having to think about it. I bet you felt better too by putting a smile on at that moment. Have you tried sharing your smile with others? It is a classic millimeter activity.

"Smile and the whole world smiles at you ..." This statement rings true, and it is so easy to do and won't cost you a penny. Do you know people who are always smiling? They seem to be chronically happy. We are naturally more attracted to people who are smiling and happy than walking around with what my mom would call a "sourpuss."

So the first step in building better relationships is to share your smile with everyone around you, strangers included. Try it for a day and you will be amazed at the smiles you get back. You will be touching so many people in such a small but significant way.

Maybe some of these people are your employees or children or the waitress who serves you coffee each morning at the local breakfast joint.

You can take this one step further and add additional millimeter steps by adding humor and laughter to your day. While I am not inherently a funny person, I can make light of a situation that might actually go the other way and become too intense. For example, in our orthodontic practice, our younger patients can get very anxious about having impressions or molds of their teeth done. We place this goopy, putty material in their mouths, and it becomes rubbery in about 60 seconds. Those 60 seconds can last an eternity in the patients' minds. Sometimes they start to gag a bit or just get very nervous. Our employees will proceed to play a game with them that takes their minds off the procedure. It is fun to watch them try to put their right legs up in the air at the same time they need to touch their noses with their left hands. The instructions continue like this until the material is set enough to be removed from their mouths. While the patient can't laugh at the time, the parents and other siblings are having fun watching the entire event take place.

Think about ways you can incorporate humor into your day-to-day interactions with your customers, family and friends.

STEP TWO: BE LIKE MY DOG, ROCKY

My dog, Rocky, is a 10-pound Shitzu, that I received as a birthday present four years ago. He is truly the best gift I have ever been given, and he demonstrates daily the millimeter approach to relationships.

When I come home from the office, tired and worn out, he is the first one to run to the door, barking and wagging his tail so excited to see me. He will then run around the kitchen in circles continuing to express his joy that his "human" is home. After that, he will follow me into my home office so I can put my bags down and then let me know it is time to either play or snuggle.

Now I am not recommending that you run around your kitchen in circles or bark and wag your tail when your favorite customer comes into your place of business. However, what I am recommending is that you show sincere enthusiasm and excitement to your customers, clients, patients, family and friends.

With a millimeter approach, this would mean greeting people with a warm smile, looking them straight in the eyes, and letting them know how happy you are to see them. The individual receiving the warm, enthusiastic and sincere greeting will feel appreciated and respected. This is the essence of the millimeter approach. In a small way, making those people around you feel important and special will make a big, long-term impact on your relationships.

STEP THREE: LISTEN, LISTEN THEN SPEAK

We all have two ears and one mouth, so in reality we should be listening twice as much as we are speaking. However, many times we are caught interrupting people in the middle of their sentences or asking someone to repeat what they just told you.

Learning to really listen and listen with intent and compassion is a key skill in building better, stronger relationships. If you have struggled with this skill in the past, I encourage you to make a real effort to develop your listening skills.

When someone is sharing their deepest thoughts with you and you are off thinking about what you are going to make for dinner, they sense your lack of focus or interest in what they have to say. It makes them feel unappreciated and disrespected. To build solid relationships with family, friends, customers, co-workers and employees, learn to stop and listen without always offering a solution. Sometimes an ear and a hug is just what the other person needed that moment to feel special and important.

The millimeter approach is to take the time to truly listen — and in listening show that you care. Try it. It can make a big impact on your relationships.

STEP FOUR: PRAISE ABUNDANTLY

Recognizing your employees, patients and family members for a job well done or for something remarkable that they have achieved is a key millimeter strategy for building better relationships.

In his book, *Why Organizational Health Trumps Everything Else in Business*, Patrick Lencioni shares how important it is to sincerely and on a regular basis recognize employees for a job well done. He explains how effective and rewarding this can be for not only the employees, but for the overall success of the business.

I have found this to be very true in our own practice with not only our employees, but our patients, too. The majority of employees in a dental office are women. These women work hard each day to deliver a service to the patients in the practice and then go home to attend to their families. Once at home, they usually start their second job, cooking dinner and helping the kids with homework. More than likely they are not getting a lot of praise at home. Not because their family does not appreciate all they are doing, but mostly because they just forget to do it.

Likewise, at our offices, we forget to give them the verbal praise they deserve.

I decided several years ago that I would verbally praise my team in front of other team members and patients. I wanted to recognize their exceptional efforts at helping a patient or parent receive care, get a question answered, or provide a solution to a problem in the practice.

At first, this was not easy for me, not because I did not want to do it, but because I would forget. The day would "fly" by, and I realized I had not praised anyone. I solved my dilemma by simply placing three pennies in the left pocket of my lab coat and making sure by the end of the day all three pennies were in my right pocket – a sign that I said three words of praise each day.

It works most days, but with a millimeter approach, I know that just one small praise given to one of my employees will give her more satisfaction and self-esteem than just about anything else I can do.

I discovered the same would work for our patients, too. Young kids and teens would often come into the office with poor oral hygiene and broken braces. Because they were not brushing after every meal as prescribed and they were eating hard candy and sticky foods, their treatment was getting behind schedule and sometimes not going anywhere at all.

We used to have a rigid policy about non-compliance and would come down hard on the patient to get him or her to see it "our" way. We decided to take a millimeter approach and handle the situation differently. Through constant and persistent education (and a lot of patience), we were able to gain the patient's trust and cooperation to get them to start committing to do what they needed to do to succeed with their braces. A millimeter at a time, we started to see improvement.

You can guess what we did. That's right, we started to praise the patient out loud for all to hear and especially in front of their mom and dad. It was incredible to see how their faces would light up, and they would continue to improve with brushing their teeth and actually stopped eating all those hard and sticky foods that were harmful to the braces.

STEP FIVE: BE THE GIVER

When it comes to giving, the millimeter approach is that even the smallest of gifts can have a big impact. Millimeter businesses are masters at giving. They often give away free gifts, products, services and information. Even if you do not have a business or even any money to spare, you can still be a giver.

The millimeter approach would be to give your time to a charity or some other organization that you are passionate about. There are so many organizations today that would welcome your time and experience.

You could give away your specialized knowledge or information that you have that would help others. With social media today, that is one way to connect and build relationships with others. You can be the one posting great information and useful resources and tips without self-promotion.

How about with your family? Can you give more than you have? For some of you reading this, this could be the toughest area. You may have come from a broken home and had some broken relationships with your parents and siblings. The millimeter approach is the best way to re-establish those relationships.

How about friends and co-workers? Do you have opportunities to be the giver and re-build those relationships? A millimeter approach would be to start with a small step, like an invite to coffee, a handwritten note or maybe a phone call. You will be amazed how you can begin to impact those broken relationships for the better.

Here are several case studies that exhibit the millimeter approach to relationships. They were willing to do what it takes to build better, long lasting and healthy relationships a millimeter at a time.

USING A MILLIMETER APPROACH TO BUILDING BETTER RELATIONSHIPS

CASE STUDY

Cari Andreani, Jacksonville, Florida

My problem in my relationship was with my mother. I grew up resenting her and rebelling as a teen. As I became an adult, the resentment I held onto poisoned my other relationships including my marriage and being a mother myself.

The steps I took to overcome included:
1. Forgiveness — I had to realize that by holding onto it wasn't hurting her, but only hurting me. I had to forgive.

2. I learned to see her with new eyes. I put myself in her shoes. She did the best she could with what she had and I tried to put myself in her shoes raising a daughter as a single parent. I am married and don't know how I could do it without my husband's help. I learned to cut her some slack.

3. I show her love when I can. My response as a teen wasn't the best, so I try to show love and patience now. I can't go back to the past, but I can from now on show my mom the love and respect she deserves.

The results: My mom and I have a WONDERFUL relationship.

We were not even on speaking terms and now we talk all the time. She spoils me and is such a good grandma to my kids. I would recommend to others the following:

First, forgive. It may be hard, but it is not impossible. It is a choice. Second, have them look at the person with new eyes and walk in their shoes. It will give a better prospective of the situation. And three, show them kindness and love. You can't stay mad at someone who is nice — be the bigger person and restore the relationship.

Mending a relationship is for your benefit not just theirs. Living in peace has no price. ∎

USING A MILLIMETER APPROACH TO BETTER RELATIONSHIPS WITH CUSTOMERS, CLIENTS OR PATIENTS

CASE STUDIES

CJ Scarlet
CEO, Roving Coach International

My name is CJ Scarlet and I am the CEO of Roving Coach International, a multinational company that coaches employees at all levels, not just the big dogs. We also gather anonymous feedback from coaching participants so leaders know what their employees need to be happy and successful, so they can better target their employee development efforts and dollars.

My story for you involves a potential client, an HR SVP, who was adamant about NOT using our services, although her SVP of Global Ops was insisting he needed us. It all came to a head one day when the HR leader called me and accused me for 15 minutes straight of unfairly using my "close friendship" with my "next-door neighbor," the Global Ops SVP.

Well, he was neither a close friend nor my neighbor, but rather than arguing with her, I simply coached her. I went through all the usual coaching stages by allowing her to express her frustration and validating her feelings throughout the exchange. I assured her I fully understood where she was coming from and why she felt that way. Then, I asked empowering questions to tease out her real concerns

(I learned that she and the Global SVP has a tense relationship and that she felt he was shoving our company down her throat). I helped her see things from a different perspective to better appreciate my intentions, and encouraged her as she found a new way to appreciate that working with us was in her employee's "best interest" — all without trying to "sell" her or defend myself. Thankfully, the HR leader was appeased and felt more in control of the decision by the time our conversation ended after 45 long minutes. Within days we had a contract to work with this major client. We worked our tails off to ensure we exceeded her expectations and at the end of the contract, she was all smiles and singing our praises. We are in the process of working on a new contract with this client for an even larger multi-national job. ∎

Jack Eberenz
Chairman of the Board
Precision Holdings of Brevard, Inc.
Franchisor for Precision Door Service

We are a nationwide franchisor and our customers are our franchisees. Our job is to make franchisees successful and happy so they pay their royalties.

About eight years ago, we had a disaster brewing. The owners and the president of the company were spending all their time hunting, fishing, playing in the Bahamas, or doing whatever else they could think of that wasn't work. It was a mess — and the franchisees were ignored and getting more than restless; they were mad.

What was the turnaround?

We took the following steps:
1. We fired the president which caused a messy battle but we had to clear the air.
2. We tackled the litigation that had built up and began to clean it up.
3. We hired a new president who understood customer service and that our franchisees were our customers.
4. He hired a new staff of knowledgeable people in the industry who could gain the respect of the franchisees.
5. We initiated surveys of all the franchisees and solicited input on what were their ideas and how we could help them.
6. In response to their issues, we began to invest in key things like a national call center so they got business they were losing.
7. We invested heavily in tools to change the lead-generation system so that it was no longer only reliant on yellow pages, but also used other avenues including a large dose of Internet marketing.
8. We invested in a new management system so their techs could use sophisticated tools to estimate, invoice and track everything.
9. We put in a system to identify and look to the future for new plans that may come up in the future.

The results started showing five years ago — and this year resulted in a standing ovation for the management team. Dozens of franchisees have either renewed for another 10 years or are lining up to do so. If your customers are unhappy, find out why. Then listen and listen carefully. Design solutions and meet with a representative group to reinforce your ideas then test the solutions and roll out to all customers with peer approval. The company is very profitable, running smoothly with a good team. It is just up to us to take some good management steps and make sure our managers have a happy and peaceful family life. ∎

IMPLEMENTING A "MILLIMETER APPROACH" IN YOUR RELATIONSHIPS:

1. How can you use a millimeter approach to motivate and inspire your employees or colleagues?
2. Are there relationships in your personal or business life that could be significantly changed by taking small millimeter steps?
3. What can you do today to improve your relationships with your family, friends, customers, clients, patients, co-workers or employees?

IT'S ALL THE SMALL STUFF

In conclusion, by reading the stories in this chapter, you can see how small, incremental but consistent efforts to praise, recognize and reward employees, a spouse or significant other, children, family members and other people in your life can have a huge impact on your relationships.

CHAPTER 13:
A MILLIMETER APPROACH TO HEALTH AND WELLNESS

"When we least expect it, life sets us a challenge to test our courage and willingness to change; at such a moment, there is no point in pretending that nothing has happened or in saying that we are not yet ready. The challenge will not wait."
— Paul Coelho, The Devil and Miss Prym

I am writing this book in 2013 when there is an epidemic of obesity, heart disease, diabetes and cancer in the United States. According to the Centers for Disease Control (CDC), 35.7 percent of all adults today are considered obese. For children and adolescents ages 2-19, 12.5 million children or 17 percent are labeled obese. Approximately $147 billion dollars a year is spent on healthcare related to obesity. These problems include heart disease, stroke, type 2 diabetes and some types of cancers.

There are a myriad of reasons for the health problems, and the industry has tried to answer the issues with a barrage of diets, diet books, gyms and fitness programs. According to the IHRSA (the International

Health, Racquet and Sports Club Association), in 2012 there were over 50 million members of health clubs in the United States alone. This generated over $20 billion in revenues for 30,000 health clubs nationwide.

Weight-loss programs are a $61 billion business — and the average American attempts a weight-loss plan at least four times in a year. With all these programs and resources, why are we losing the "battle" of better health and wellness?

I believe the answer lies in a millimeter approach to improving your health, fitness and overall wellness. Let me explain.

I was very lucky to be raised in a family that did not have a lot of extra money to spend on going out to eat, fast food and sugary treats. Dessert at our house consisted of fruit or the occasional bowl of ice cream. We did not eat fast food. My mom, a woman of Italian descent, enjoyed cooking and did a great job especially with all things Italian. We had the occasional pizza night, but we were not fed McDonald's or Burger King. I have nothing against those restaurants, however, there are enough studies that indicate that our waistlines grow as we consume fast food. This has happened in countries outside the United States, such as China and Europe, when they too start eating a more western diet.

So honestly, throughout most of my life, I have not had a weight problem. Love me or hate me, that is the truth. However, I did gain some excess weight during my pregnancy with my first child and was surprised by how slowly the weight came off after her birth. I remember a conversation I had with a friend, when I told her how frustrated I was with how slowly I was losing the "baby" weight. She said something to me that stuck with me forever. "Donna, it took nine months to get that weight on your body, give it at least nine months to get it off."

Okay, so I was being impatient about it, but I was working hard to get my pre-pregnancy figure back. For those of you reading this that are moms and have struggled with post-pregnancy weight loss, it can seem like an eternity before you are back in your pre-baby jeans. My friend in her brilliance was right. It took some time to gain the weight, why on Earth did I think I would lose it all in one month?

But that is the way most of us view weight loss, fitness or an overhaul of our health. We want results fast, like yesterday! However, the problems we have today with too much weight and associated health problems like high-blood pressure and diabetes, did not show up overnight. It was a slow and gradual process. You gain a few pounds over the holidays and vow to shed the pounds in the New Year. You join the gym and plan to go every day for an hour and do that for the first three weeks of January and by the end of March you are barely there one time a week. Summer vacation at the beach — and you add on a few more pounds, but promise once the kids are back in school, you will get back to the gym. You go all out at the first kickboxing class and injure yourself and can't get back into the gym for another six weeks. In the meantime, another five to 10 pounds are added and then you find yourself heading into the holidays 20 pounds overweight from last year.

The cycle repeats itself year after year, until you get to the point that you give up and say that it is no use trying to lose the weight. You convince yourself that you cannot do it because now it seems like such a big mountain to climb.

Stop that talk right now!

Let's talk millimeters!

MILLIMETER WEIGHT LOSS

You did not gain all that weight quickly. It was a slow process, you could almost say it happened little by little. I am here to tell you: You can lose that weight in the same way, little by little. Stop trying to lose 20 pounds in 20 days. You did not gain it that way, why would you think you could possibly lose it that fast and stay healthy? Using a millimeter approach to improving your health and wellness will bring about small changes that if done consistently and with a plan in place, you can change the direction of your health and wellness.

I am not going to recommend a specific diet plan or fitness program for you. What I do recommend is that you find a program that fits your lifestyle and is reasonable for you to do. For example, programs that require you to buy their food may be a perfect choice for you. You might be a person who does not like to cook and would prefer to have everything ready to heat up. However, for some people, these types of programs can be cost prohibitive.

There is so much information available online regarding healthy eating, preparation of healthy meals, and what are your best food choices. My goal here is not to set a plan for you, but to get you to think about making small changes each day and following through on a program that works for you.

You might remember the young man, Jared, who lost a ton of weight eating Subway™ turkey sandwiches for a year. He has since become a well-paid spokesperson for that restaurant chain. I am not suggesting you should eat Subway™ to lose weight. Jared was consistent in what he did and the results were that he lost the weight he was determined to lose.

Likewise, if you start a fitness program, whether it is at a gym or even in the comfort of your home, if you have not been exercising on a regular basis it is probably not a good idea to start with the most advanced workouts and do them every day. Besides being extremely sore and tired, you could injure yourself and not be able to work out for weeks. Start off slowly and at the beginner levels and work your way up to the advanced and five-days-a-week workouts.

STEPS TOWARD FITNESS

I will share a personal story that happened recently with my husband. We both do a workout called Crossfit™. It is an advanced workout that combines aerobics, gymnastics, Olympic-style weight lifting and some other fairly challenging moves and exercises. While many of the members are extremely experienced athletes, there are plenty of us who do this workout because it is fun, challenging, motivating and always different. The workouts are scaled up or down depending on what you feel comfortable doing and how much you want to be challenged.

My husband has not been a been fan of organized workouts, but when he started Crossfit™ he became hooked. Besides getting him into great physical shape, he lost 20 pounds that he had been trying to lose since I was pregnant with our second child (spouses gain baby weight too). About 12 months into the workouts, he hurt his back by lifting weights that were probably too advanced for him — and that put him out of the gym for three months.

Guess what happened? Yep, 20 pounds of weight back on his body. Fortunately, his back healed and he is back doing Crossfit™ again, but this time, respecting his back and body and making sure not to go overboard and lift too much weight or do an exercise that might strain his back.

Hey, we have all been there and experienced setbacks on our goals to improve our fitness, weight and overall health.

WEIGHT LOSS IN MILLIMETERS

CASE STUDY

**Debbie Johnson,
best-selling author of Think Yourself Thin**

I gained forty pounds dieting, lost it all thinking thin, and have kept it off for over 25 years! I got so fed up with gaining weight by dieting that I gave it up. Then I said to myself, "Well, if this is how I'm supposed to look, so be it!" I woke up the next morning, after accepting my fate, and realized I could use all the positive thinking and imaging principles I'd developed to be successful in business! What small steps did I take to lose the weight? Since I'd gained weight from dieting, I stopped doing that and started thinking like a thin person. I said to myself every morning before even getting out of bed, "I feel a little bit thinner today." I acted "as if" I was getting thinner each day — and I did!

It took two years to accomplish my goal. The only problem I faced was that I thought I might get too thin, but that never happened. I've kept the weight off over 25 years. The most useful piece of advice, change your self-image immediately and work on imagining yourself slim. Do it daily. Love yourself and be patient through the process. It took me a lot longer to lose the weight than it did to gain it, as I gained it quickly after each diet. Know that you will keep it off much longer this way! I eat whatever I want because my body is stabilized and my subconscious program is reset. ∎

HEALTH IN MILLIMETERS

How about improving your family's health a millimeter at a time. As an orthodontist, I see children all day long with many health-related problems that could be solved or at least improved through better eating habits and some exercise.

Childhood obesity is an enormous health problem. Obese children and adolescents are more likely to have cardiovascular disease, type 2 diabetes, joint and bone problems, sleep apnea, and social and psychological problems due to low self-esteem from the excess weight. They also are more likely to get many different types of cancers including, breast, ovarian, colon, lung, kidney, prostrate, myeloma and Hodgkin's disease.

These are all preventable problems that can be solved taking a millimeter approach.

I will share how we made some changes in our family's diet.

My grandparents (all four of them) were diabetic. They became diabetic later in life as adults. None of them were overweight, however, they did eat a very high-carbohydrate diet, especially lots of pasta as is traditional for Italians. My grandfather's diabetes was not well controlled, and I remember him losing part of his leg to gangrene when I was just in junior high. At the time I did not quite understand how it happened except for the fact that he was diabetic and had poor circulation. You can bet, after that I wanted to know how you became diabetic and if it could be prevented. Sugar is a big factor in diabetes. My mom was not a big dessert person and became even more conscious of the sugar in our diets after my grandfather had his amputation.

With two teenage children now in our household, we were experiencing some interesting health issues. Our daughter was having a terrible time with acne. It was so bad on her back that it often would ooze and cause her pain. We tried some homeopathic topical ointments and other over-the-counter topical medications. They would work, but it was a temporary solution, as it would come back in a few weeks.

In my research to help her without going to a dermatologist, I discovered that eliminating sugar and increasing water intake could solve her problem. She loves her sweets, and she has a huge sweet tooth. The first thing I did was get rid of all the sweets in the house. Cookies, ice cream, candy, sugar cereals and breads were removed and not purchased again. Next I bought her a one-liter BPA-free water bottle and had her drink at least three liters a day of water.

It took less than a month for all her acne on her back and face to disappear forever. She noticed the change and told me the other day she bought a cookie at school and she could not finish it as it almost made her sick. Small changes in her diet reaped big rewards that will help her not only with her acne, but also with her overall health and wellness.

Our son had a similar problem with severe seasonal allergies, especially in the spring.

He would get red eyes, sore throat, and a stuffy nose and cough usually in the spring. Sometimes it would get so severe that he could not go outside for recess at school. At home, he would often sit inside because being outside would cause him to have trouble breathing, and he would break into a horrible coughing spell.

I did some research on my own and ended up taking him to a chiropractor, who tested him for different types of allergens. The typical ones in the springtime near our house were confirmed. He was allergic to those. What was really interesting is that we discovered he was extremely allergic to sugar. If he was eating a lot of sugary foods, the allergies would get even worse. Despite his complaints about it, we eliminated as much refined sugar from his diet as we could. We started to slowly see improvements in his health — and he no longer needed the allergy medication.

He began to feel better too, and he naturally began to understand that if he went back to eating sugar, he would start to feel sick again. Keeping him away from sugar became easier once he started to feel better. Today, he consumes sugar on a very limited basis especially in the spring, when the other allergens are in full force.

It is amazing how the body can heal itself, by making some small, but significant changes in your diet or even lifestyle.

Here is another story where a small change in diet or lifestyle made a big impact.

WEIGHT LOSS IN MILLIMETERS

CASE STUDY

Joanie Jacobsen
http://babyboomerway.com

I am a 60-year-old woman who initially lost 60 pounds in 14 months (3/09-5/10). For me the struggle was to alter my mindset. I wanted to be able to move forward and revamp my entire lifestyle. I had tried many different diets and ways to lose weight but would always revert back to my bad habits after I was successful, which caused me to gain more weight. I would have to break this behavior if I was to remain fit and healthy. One of the first steps I took was to eat a salad and try to incorporate at least 30 minutes of exercise each day. I tried it for 21 days (the salad and exercise) and it became a habit. I increased my exercise intensity and time and ate a low-fat diet as well as the salad. A blood test from my doctor showed I was heading toward high-blood pressure and type 2 diabetes.

My setbacks were losing three family members and my full-time job in the last 18 months, which sent me off track, therefore I gained about 18 pounds. I am now following the same path that helped me initially. My tip would be to take baby steps toward a fit-and-healthy lifestyle by changing your mindset, thinking positive, and always having a goal in mind (mine was to wear a bathing suit in public). ∎

That is the key to success in improving your health. You do not need to spend hundreds or even thousands of dollars on a fancy diet program or the latest gym equipment. Set a goal to lose the weight or get in better shape. Rather than committing to large weight-loss goals, set a small but significant goal that you know you can and will achieve.

Likewise, if your goal is to get to the gym on a regular basis or just exercise more or improve your family's diet, do it with a millimeter approach.

Make those small changes, be consistent, and reap the rewards of better health for the rest of your life.

IMPLEMENTING A "MILLIMETER APPROACH" TO HEALTH AND WELLNESS:

1. What health issue are you struggling with right now?
2. Could you use a millimeter approach to improve your health?
3. What small, millimeter changes can you make today that would start you on the path to better health and wellness?

CHAPTER 14:
CHANGING YOUR MINDSET WITH A MILLIMETER APPROACH

"Some changes look negative on the surface but you will soon realize that space is being created in your life for something new to emerge."
— Eckhart Tolle

This final chapter is probably the most important when it comes to making the millimeter changes needed to make the big impact in your business and life. Honestly, unless you have the right mindset to take a millimeter approach to change, you will continue along the same path. As Albert Einstein said, "Insanity is doing the same thing over and over again and expecting different results."

So what is the definition of mindset? Mindset is a habitual or characteristic mental attitude that determines how you will interpret and respond to situations. For example, you have a new software system at work and you immediately think that it will have problems and not be as good as the previous system. You let everyone in the office know you are not happy about the change. In your mind, you are saying to yourself that you do not like when the boss changes things, and therefore you have decided already that the new system will be a failure.

Mindset can also be your beliefs about yourself and your abilities.

For example, if one of your co-workers is having a party and everyone is talking about it, but you have not received the invitation yet, you might be thinking, "I never get invited to these fun events, I guess I am just boring" (or a loser, or not with the in-crowd ...). Your mindset is one that assumes you were not invited and something is wrong with you. You may also take a different approach and say to yourself, "Well, I didn't want to go to that party anyway. All the office backstabbers will be there!"

Another example of a poor mindset is when you attempt to do something, like implement a new marketing strategy for your business. You have spent the money, got the website up and all the social media sites, and you are ready to sit back and wait for the phone to ring. And guess what? It doesn't.

What would you say to yourself?

What would you do next?

You have a certain mindset about your abilities, intelligence and personality. Your mindset however can be one of two things. You can have a fixed mindset. What that means is you believe you have a level of intelligence, certain talents and a personality type that cannot be changed. You were essentially "born this way."

Hopefully, because you have read through this book, you are in the second category, and you believe that you have certain abilities and a personality type that can be improved upon or enhanced. You believe in personal development and lifelong learning. You have the mindset that you are constantly looking to improve either in your level of understanding a particular topic or field or becoming better at a specific skill such as business, management, parenting, acting, singing, teaching, public speaking or writing.

This "growth" mindset believes they develop their specific qualities through determination, dedication, persistence and continual effort. They understand that no one has ever accomplished great things — not Mozart, Michelangelo, or Michael Jordan — without years of focused practice and learning. Alfred Binet, the inventor of the IQ test was a big believer that learning, implementation and practice could bring about fundamental changes in intelligence. Most people believed his IQ test was developed to categorize children's unchangeable intelligence.

On the contrary, in one of his books, *Modern Ideas About Children*, he writes, "A few modern philosophers assert that an individual's intelligence is a fixed quantity, a quantity which cannot be increased. We must protest and react against this brutal pessimism. With practice, training and above all, method, we manage to increase our attention, our memory, our judgment and literally to become more intelligent than we were before."

Scientists are learning that people have the capacity to learn and develop their brains as they age. People may have a certain start to their education process, but with access to information that they want to use to develop new skills and talents, they can succeed. Their success is dependent on their efforts and determination to take the information and learn it, use it, and take action on it. Robert Sternberg, a present-day guru on intelligence, writes that the major factor in whether people achieve expertise "is not some fixed prior ability, but purposeful engagement." In other words, the people who take action will succeed.

So in this final chapter, let's take a look at how we can take a millimeter approach to changing your mindset from being stuck and thinking things like:

"I can't do this."

"I'm not smart enough."

"I'm not disciplined enough."

"I do not have any real talent."

"I am too old to change or learn."

"I have tried that before and it did not work."

"I do not have the time or energy to make the changes."

You can fill in your specific objection in case I missed it!

I do not remember exactly where I heard this term, but it has stuck with me through the years. I use it quite often with my teenaged children when they need a mindset adjustment. I am going to use it here to help you with a similar need.

Please stop your "stinking thinking!"

Okay, there, I said it!

I promise to leave you with some tips on how to get rid of your "stinking thinking" and get your butt off the couch and start working a millimeter at a time.

SETBACKS AREN'T THE END OF THE WORLD

First, you need to learn to deal with potential setbacks.

When you begin the journey, even a millimeter approach will have setbacks. Your inner voice may say, "See I told you. You were not smart enough or good enough or talented enough to do this...what were you thinking?"

With the right mindset in place, you will understand that making the changes in your business or life are part of your growth process.

You know it has nothing to do with your innate intelligence or abilities, but more to do with your persistence and determination to succeed.

Secondly, recognize that you have control over your success.

If you interpret your setbacks, criticisms and other challenges as indicators that you are a failure, then you will be a failure. On the other hand, if you interpret your setbacks, criticisms and challenges as part of your growth strategy that will stretch you and expand your comfort zone and your abilities, then you will reap the positive benefits of that mindset.

Finally, focus on personal growth and development as a lifelong opportunity.

People are living longer, fuller lives today and many are embarking on second and third careers. Instead of looking at change as scary or viewing growth and education as burdensome, look at it as an adventure, full of fun and new experiences. Benjamin Barber, an eminent sociologist, once said, "I don't divide the world into weak and the strong, or the successes and the failures...I divide the world into the learners and non-learners."

We start early in life learning so much. We learn to walk first by crawling and then standing and taking our first few steps. We spend many days or weeks stepping and falling until we can get it right. As a baby we did not worry about falling or making a mistake. We just get up and do it again and again.

FAIL TO SUCCEED

When did we start caring about making mistakes and failing? This entire book has been about growing, succeeding and changing your life. I will be the first to admit, change is scary. It is also hard to do. That is why a millimeter approach, one small step at a time toward your goals, whether they be business related or personal, will allow you to make those changes. These small, millimeter steps when done consistently and with determination, will help you achieve your goals and make a huge impact in your business and life.

The real truth about ability and achievement can be illustrated by this story about Thomas Edison.

Thomas Edison is famous for being a great inventor. His most significant invention was the development of a practical incandescent electric light. The idea for electric lighting was not new, and a number of people had worked on and even developed different prototypes. Edison was the first to develop an incandescent light bulb, and eventually an electrical lighting system. The first commercial power station was located in New York City and opened in September, 1882. This was the start of the electric age.

Many people think Thomas Edison worked alone, holed up in his workshop like some mad scientist. The truth is he was not a loner. In fact, for the invention of the incandescent light bulb, he had 30 assistants, including well-trained scientists, often working around the clock in a corporate-funded state-of-the-art laboratory. The invention of the light bulb and commercial electric power did not happen overnight. In fact, the incandescent light bulb was invented by an entire network of smaller, time-consuming inventions each requiring one or more chemists, mathematicians, physicists, engineers and glass blowers.

Edison himself, while universally given credit for the invention of the light bulb and the "electric age," relied on a team of co-workers to help him. He was the face of the invention because of his drive and mindset to succeed. "I speak without exaggeration when I say that I have constructed 3,000 different theories in connection with the electric light, each one of them reasonable and apparently likely to be true."
— Thomas Edison

My purpose in sharing this story is twofold.

One, Edison was not a boy genius, but a driven individual with the mindset that success was his. He knew it was a matter of trying and trying again, before he would get it right. In his lifetime, he is credited for 1,093 different inventions. At what point in the 2,999 attempts to develop a safe and practical incandescent light bulb would you have quit? After two failed attempts? Maybe a dozen? How many times have you given up or stopped trying after just one failed attempt?

I admit, it would be tough to continue after even 20 attempts with no success. However, Thomas Edison took a millimeter approach to solving the problem of creating a practical and useful light source that we all enjoy today. He may not have realized it was a millimeter approach, but can you imagine what our lives would be like today if he did not keep going until he found the solution?

The second point that illustrates his ability to succeed is that he had a team in place. He had people to help him. He was not alone. So many of us attempt to make changes without a support team in place. Get a team in place. Tell your family, spouse, significant other or close friends what you are planning to do.

Do you plan to lose that weight once and for all? Then get a partner to help keep you accountable or go on walks with you every day. Are you wanting to take your business in a new direction but are feeling unsure of the direction? Then by all means seek out a business coach, consultant, CPA or other trusted advisor to help you.

The millimeter approach is not for loners. The small changes that you will make consistently, while small, may need someone to help you over the rougher spots or give you the encouragement that you need.

I have an extremely supportive spouse and my two teenage children are my best cheerleaders. There are days when I feel inadequate, stupid and downright depressed. We all have those days, and all it takes to get you back on your "millimeter" path is a word of encouragement or just a good old-fashioned hug. Find those special people to help you and likewise be that person for someone in your life looking to take a millimeter approach to change.

My wish for you, my reader, is that you follow your dreams, live this gift you have, your life, to the fullest.

CONCLUSION

"An ounce of action is worth a ton of theory."
— Ralph Waldo Emerson

This book is about change.

If you Google the word "change" to search for its definition, it is a verb that means to make or become different. Change can also be a noun, in which it becomes the act of instance or making or becoming different.

Finally, there are many synonyms for change, my favorite being the word transform. If we take the word change and replace it with transform, you can begin to feel the empowerment that change can bring to your business and your life. But change can be scary. Change can seem impossible. Change can make you feel vulnerable.

What is stopping you from making the changes needed in your business or life? What prevents you from taking the steps to begin your transformation? Do you have any of these excuses?

1. If I try and fail, I will be embarrassed in front of my friends, family and co-workers.
2. If I make the changes I want to, the people around me may not know me anymore or I may lose their friendship.

3. I feel overwhelmed just trying to make it through the day, let alone trying to make significant changes in my business or life.
4. I really don't believe in my ability to change my life or business.
5. I am worried about what others will think about me.
6. I do not know where to start. There are too many changes I need to make and I feel overwhelmed.
7. I do not have a strong support system in place to help me through the transformation I would like to do in my business or life.

Do you relate to any of these above statements? For some of you reading this you may have said "yes" to all seven excuses. While you make excuses and believe change is scary, impossible, and leaves you feeling vulnerable, you now know that it can happen a millimeter at a time. Most people who set out to make some changes in their businesses or personal lives do it in a BIG way. They set their sights on huge goals and massive action. I am not saying that big goals and massive action will not work. THEY WILL!

You can have those big goals and succeed. By now you should know the answer.

The millimeter approach to change or transformation is less scary, less overwhelming and less insurmountable. Small steps, done consistently and on purpose can make a big impact on your business or life. Throughout this book you have read stories about how we transformed our practice into a bigger and better one by focusing on the millimeter changes we could make. You have also read about other businesses as well as personal stories about how they used millimeters to transform their businesses and personal lives.

Millimeters are an extremely small measurement. In the beginning of this book, I shared how important millimeters are in my profession of dentistry. Millimeters are our primary measuring tool for evaluating success or failure in the dental or orthodontic work we do. With that prospective, I have learned that it is truly the small millimeter changes that when done consistently and over time, will transform a patient's smile, turn around a business heading for disaster, mend broken relationships, empower employees, and help individuals grow into admirable leaders.

The millimeter approach is also about taking the time to look at the small things in our businesses and lives. These small "things" could be an interaction with a customer, client or patient, a kind word to a stranger at the mall, a public praise to an employee for a job well done, or a special gift or outing as a surprise for a spouse or child. I am constantly amazed through my daily efforts to praise and recognize my patients, employees, family and even complete strangers, how I can impact their lives in a small millimeter way. My reward is a huge smile and knowing that I impacted their lives as well as mine by using a millimeter approach.

My final wish for you is that you start today using a millimeter approach to finally make those changes in your business or life. Change can happen a millimeter at a time.

Now that you know you can take a "millimeter approach" to the changes you want and need to make in your business and your life, I have put together a FREE workbook to help you achieve your goals. Download instantly my **FREE Workbook,** *It's All About Millimeters: Making The Small Changes To Achieve The Big Impact in Your Business and Your Life.* Go to **drdonnagalante.com** to get started today to make those small, but significant changes.

****

ACKNOWLEDGMENTS

There are so many people who have impacted my career as an orthodontist and practice owner. First of all, I want to thank everyone who has been a teacher or mentor to me through college, dental school and even my orthodontic residency program.

In particular, Dr. Ed Marcus from the University of Pennsylvania School of Dental Medicine who was my "Group Leader" during my two years in the clinic. He guided me to become an excellent clinical dentist and was grooming me for a career as a prosthodontist. I know he was a bit upset when I told him I was going to specialize in orthodontics.

Dr. Robert Vanarsdall, the Chairman of the Department of Orthodontics at University of Pennsylvania who accepted me into his program right out of dental school and inspired me to become the orthodontist I am today. Other professors that I wish to thank include, Dr. David Musich, Dr. Marion Doyle, Dr. Peter Greco, Dr. Chip Forward and Dr. Harvey Levitt, all of whom were instrumental in helping me both professionally and personally. I had the privilege of working with the late Dr. Barney Swain both as his student and then as his associate for several years in his practice in Morristown, NJ. It was an honor to be around one of the giants in the field of orthodontics, and I was lucky to have had that opportunity. He taught me how to be humble and gracious under any circumstance and not let your ego get in the way of your success.

As a freshly minted orthodontist with loads of student debt, I am forever grateful to Dr. Fred Ferrari for our association for many years in his Flemington, NJ office. His entire family adopted me as their own and I began to understand the business side of dentistry while in his office.

Over the years, I have had numerous mentors — some I have met in person and others have taught me through their books, audios and DVD's. To all of them, I say, "thank you" and will mention a few who in particular helped me enormously. They are: Dan Kennedy, Michael Gerber, Brian Tracy, Jay Conrad Levinson, Ali Brown, Zig Ziglar, Napoleon Hill, Jim Rohn, Chet Holmes, Seth Godin, John Maxwell, Brendon Burchard, Joe Polish, John Wooden, Bo Eason and Jay Abraham. Many of these people have books that should be part of your personal development library.

Thank you to my publisher, Michelle Gamble at 3L Publishing. She kept me on task to get this book done. Without her kind, but persistent emails reminding me of when she would receive the next chapter, I am not sure if this book would have ever been completed. Erin Pace-Molina, Bo Bradley and the rest of the team at 3L Publishing, thank you for all you do to get authors like myself published.

I am grateful to our team of professionals at Cater Galante Orthodontics. They work hard every day to help our patients receive amazing care and stunning smiles. They are always willing to try a new technique, change a system that is not working anymore, or introduce a new product or service. The "millimeter" approach is alive and well in our offices and our team makes it look easy.

ACKNOWLEDGMENTS

My husband, Dr. Paul Cater, who constantly encourages me and is always willing to implement my crazy ideas for over 19 years now; I am grateful for his constant love and support. He never gives up on me and he is my biggest cheerleader.

And last, but by no means least, I am grateful to all the patients and parents who have entrusted us with the care of their children smiles or their own smiles. It has been an honor and privilege to be a part of your lives.

My personal reward in publishing this book is that you will be inspired and motivated to make those changes in either your business, professional practice or personal life. Now go, make a big impact … a millimeter at a time.

I would love to hear from you about how you used some of the ideas in my book to impact your business, professional practice or personal life. Please share your story and email me at drdonna@drdonnagalante.com.

ABOUT THE AUTHOR

Dr. Donna Galante has been a practicing orthodontist for over 27 years. A graduate of the University of Pennsylvania School of Dental Medicine, she received both her dental degree and Orthodontic Specialty certification at the Ivy League School. While there, she received the Henry Goldman Award for Clinical Excellence and the Orthodontic Department Research Award.

For eight years she was a part-time, clinical instructor in the Department of Orthodontics at the University of Pennsylvania and also started her first private practice in King of Prussia, Pennsylvania. She was voted twice as the Instructor of the Year by the graduate students in the Orthodontic Department.

In 1993 she sold her practice and moved to California to get married and start her family. Since that time she and her husband, Dr. Paul Cater, also an orthodontist, have started five practices, bought three practices, and sold three practices. They currently have four practice locations in Northern California.

Their practices are in the top one percent of revenue of all orthodontic practices nationwide and have won several local awards such as "Best of the Best Orthodontists" from the readers of Placer Herald Newspapers in 2009 and 2012.

Dr. Galante has been voted twice by her peers as a top orthodontist in the Sacramento area (2011, 2012).

Besides her practice commitments, she has a separate coaching company that specializes in helping women dentists and specialists succeed in their professional and personal lives. As a wife, practice owner, mother, sister, daughter, aunt, friend and businesswomen, she understands the demands that are placed on dentists, especially women, who are juggling a multitude of commitments and responsibilities.

Her biggest thrill is when she has a client begin using her millimeter approach, and he or she experiences huge changes in his or her practice that ultimately lead to more happiness and fulfillment professionally and personally.

She is a highly sought out speaker and has co-authored several other books, *Big Ideas for Your Business* by America's Premier Experts and *Power Principles for Success* that she co-authored with Brian Tracy. She also wrote *Healthy and Beautiful at Any Age: Your Smile and Modern Orthodontics*, which helps patients and parents understand all that orthodontics has to offer today.

Further resources are available at her website
www.drdonnagalante.com

Go to www.drdonnagalante.com to get your free downloadable workbook, It's All About Millimeters: Making The Small Changes To Achieve The Big Impact in Your Business and Your Life